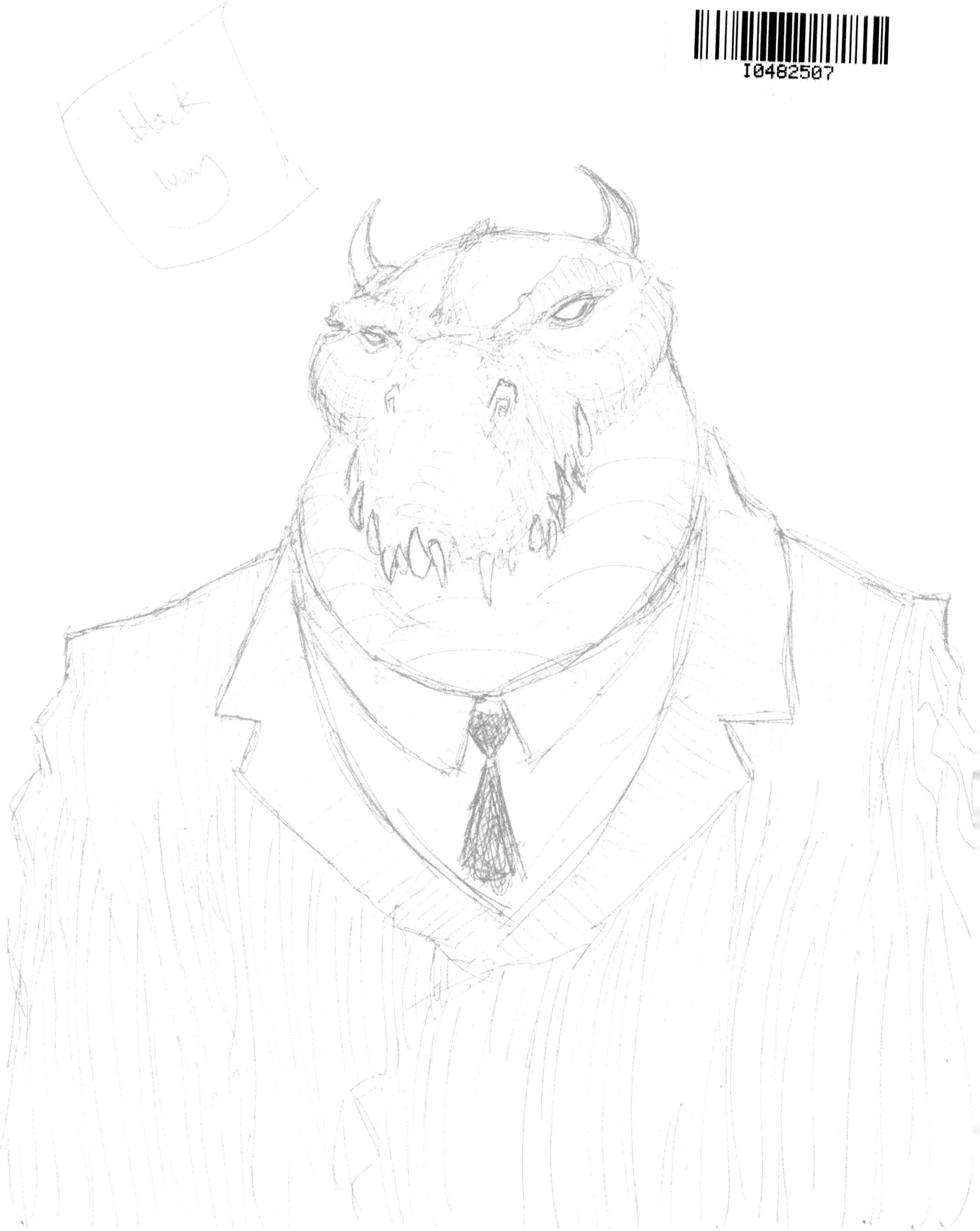
black lung

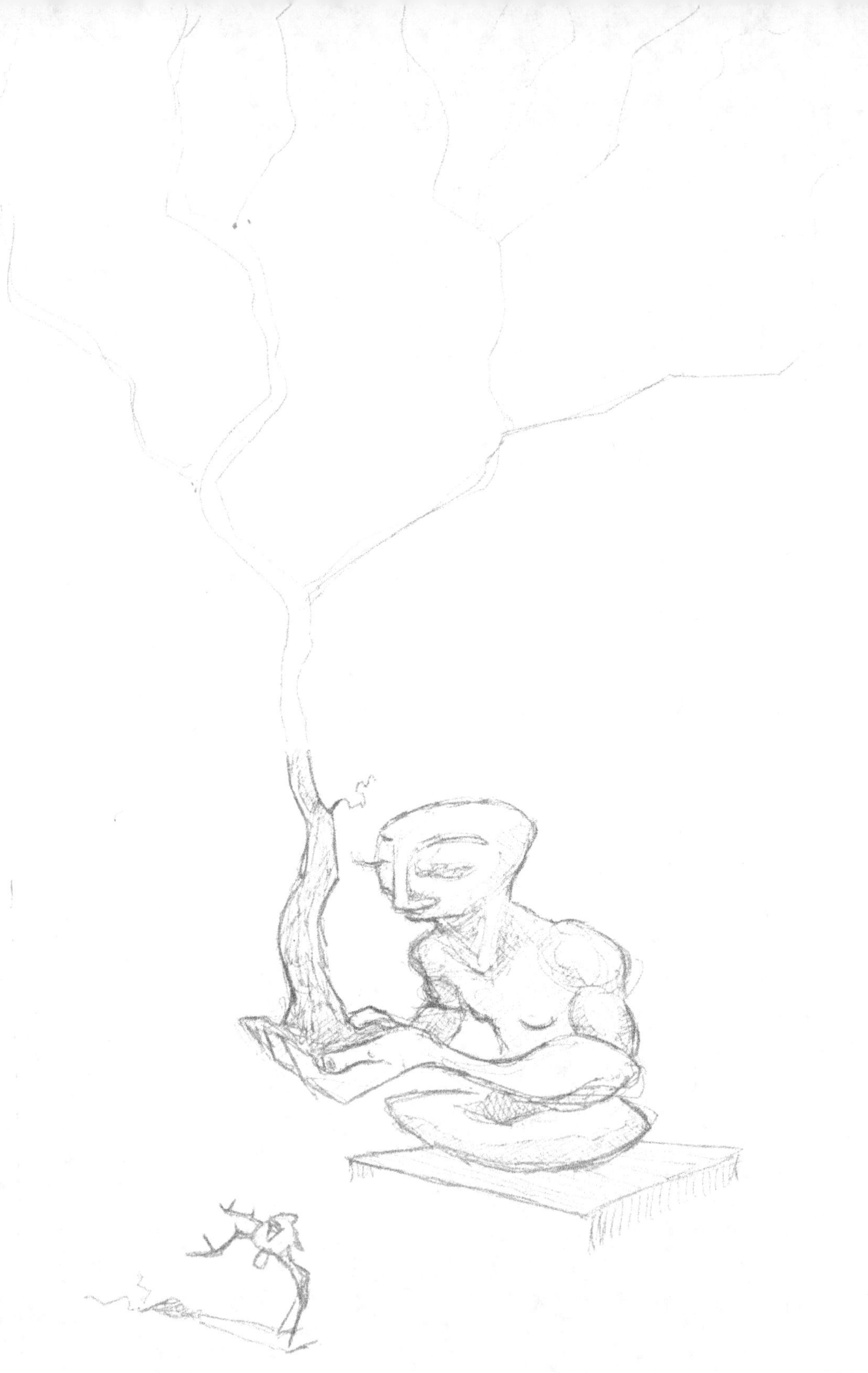

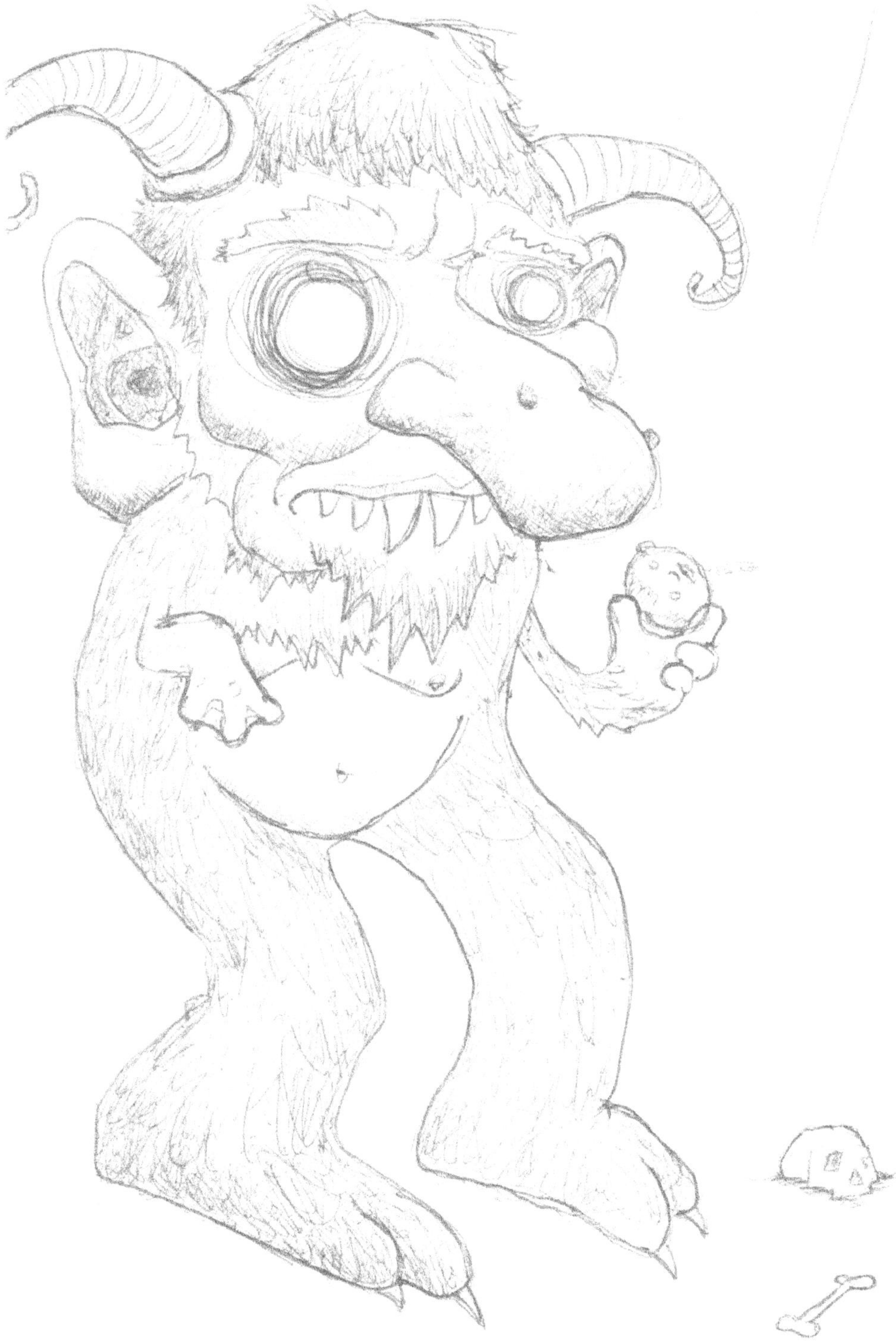

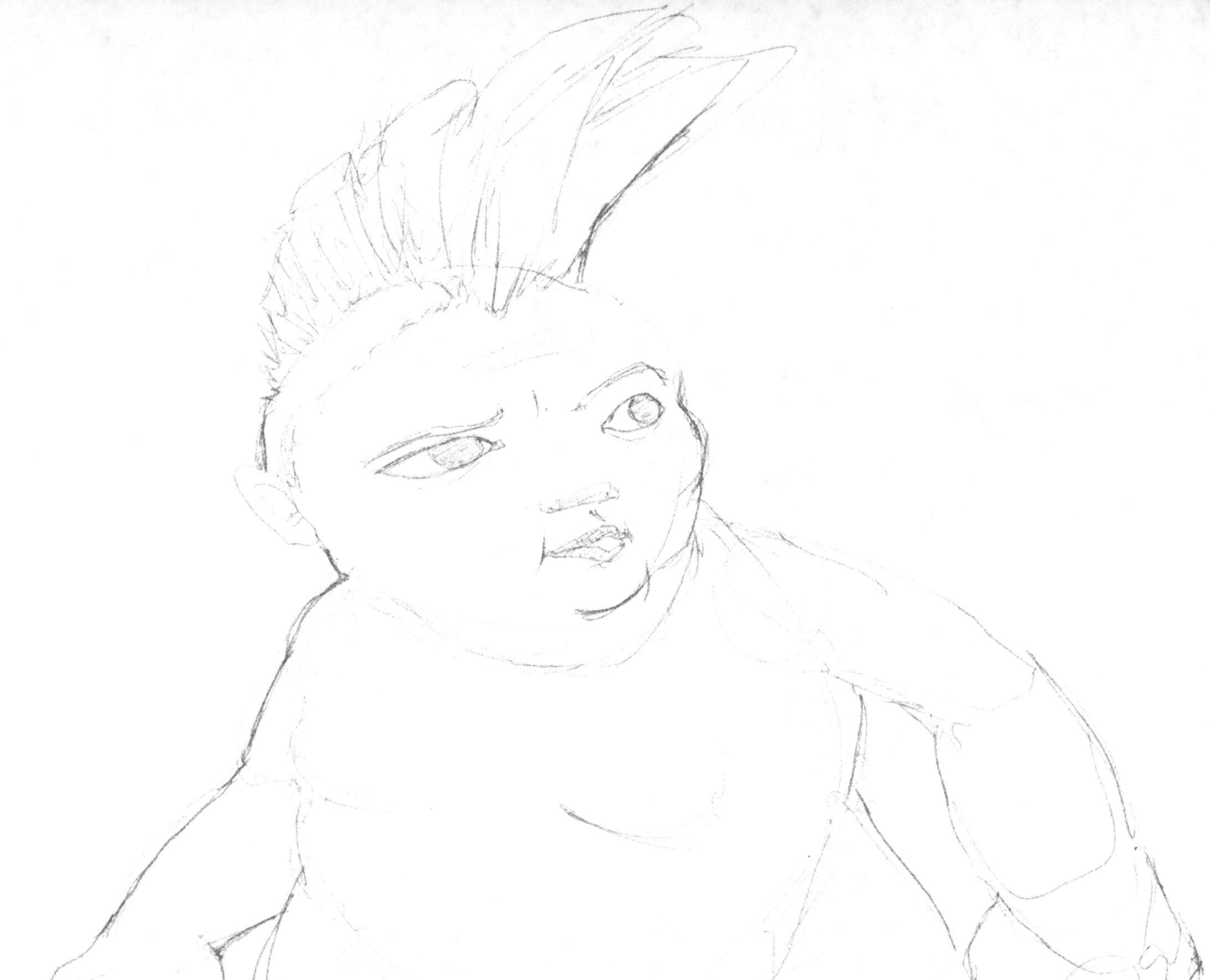

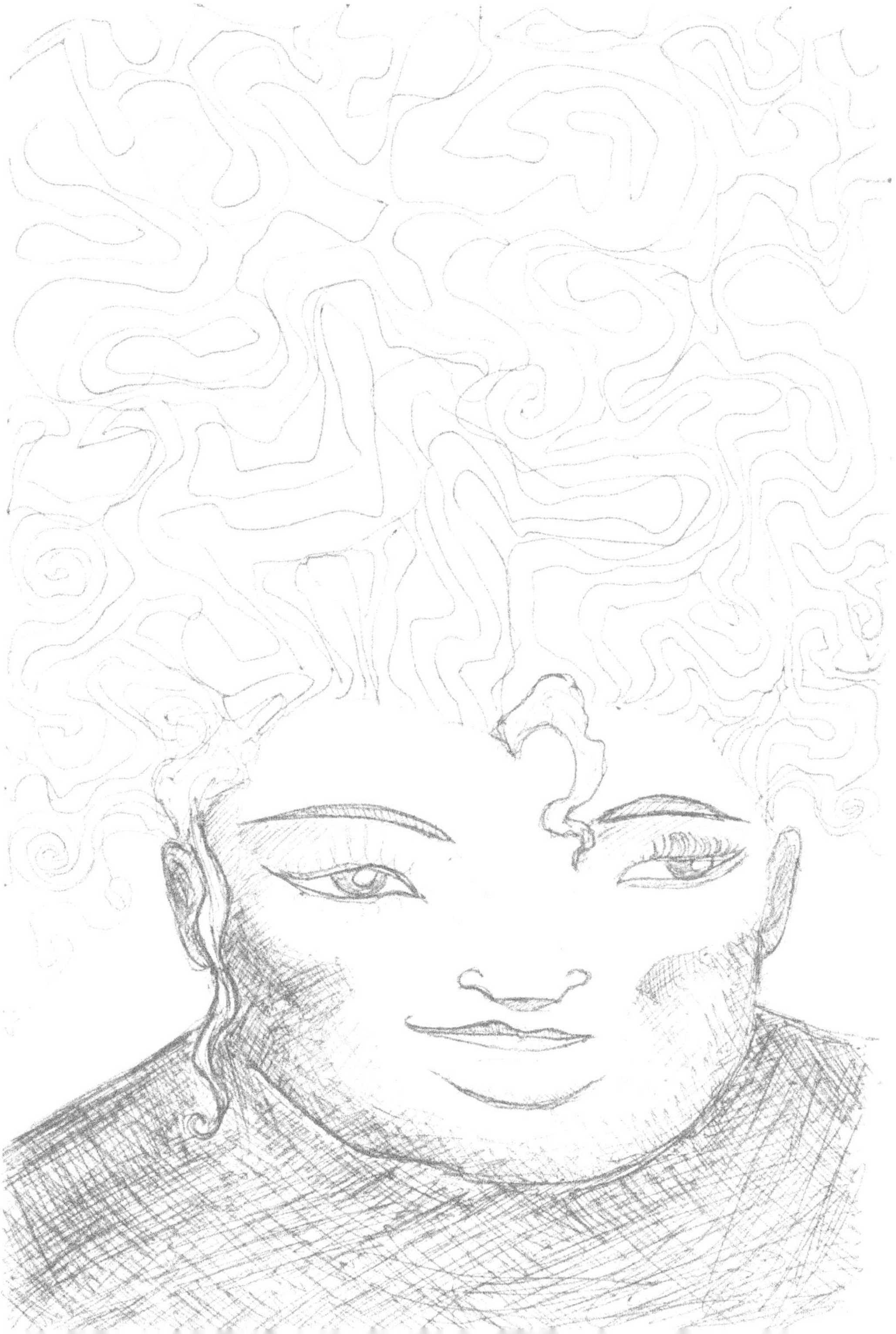

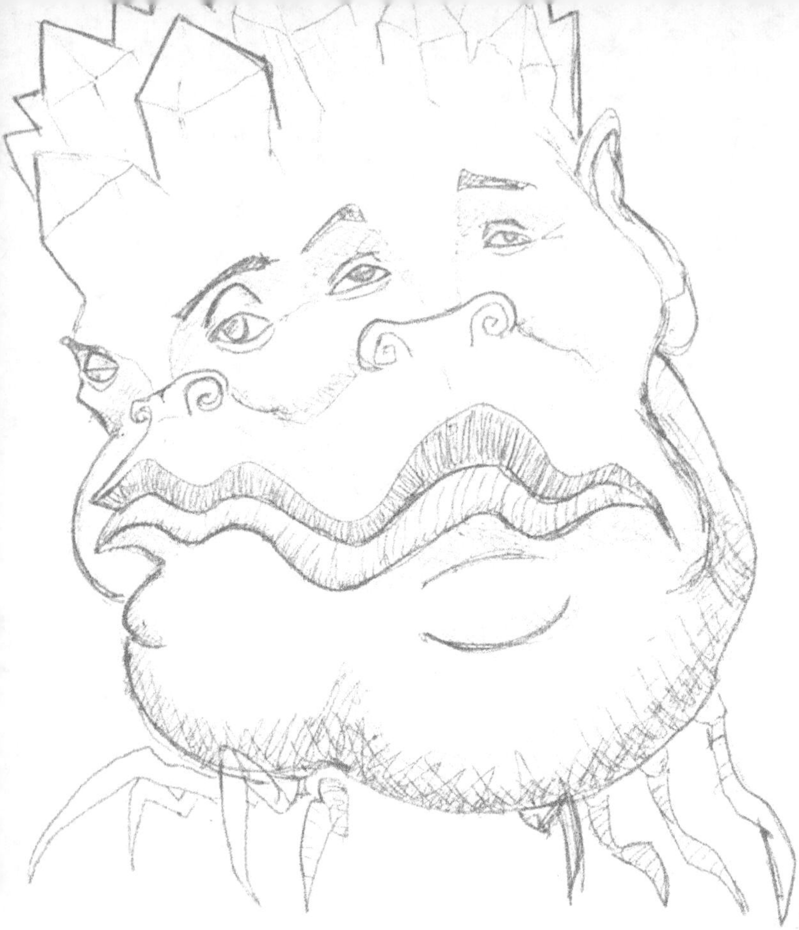

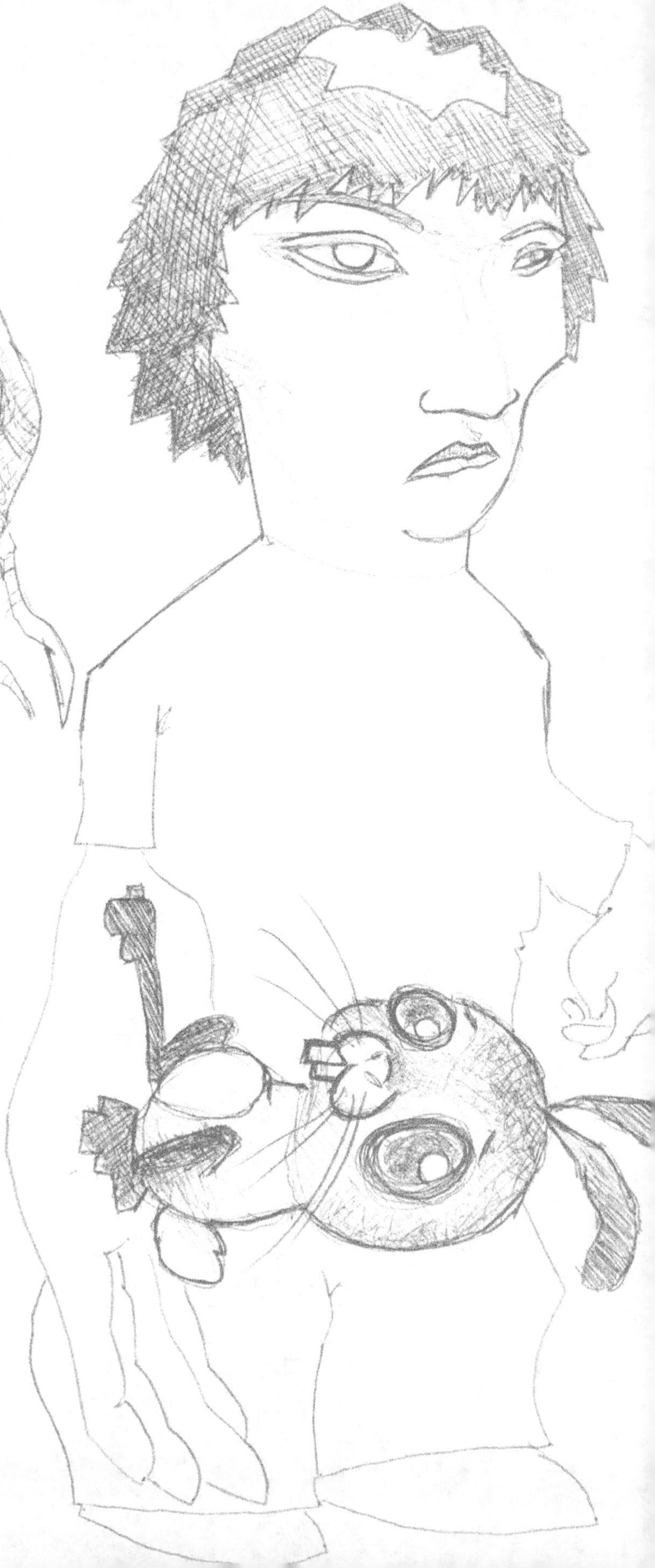

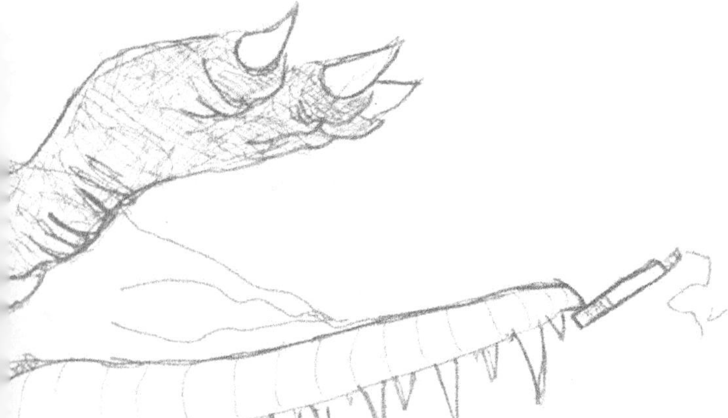

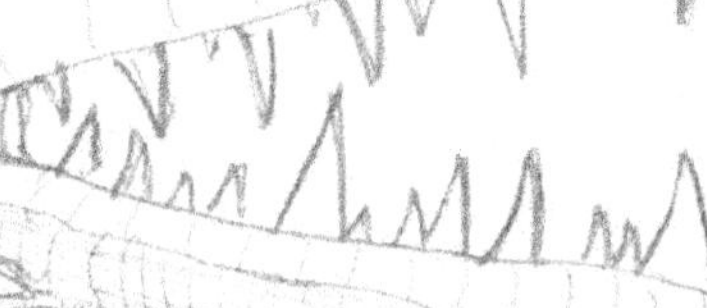

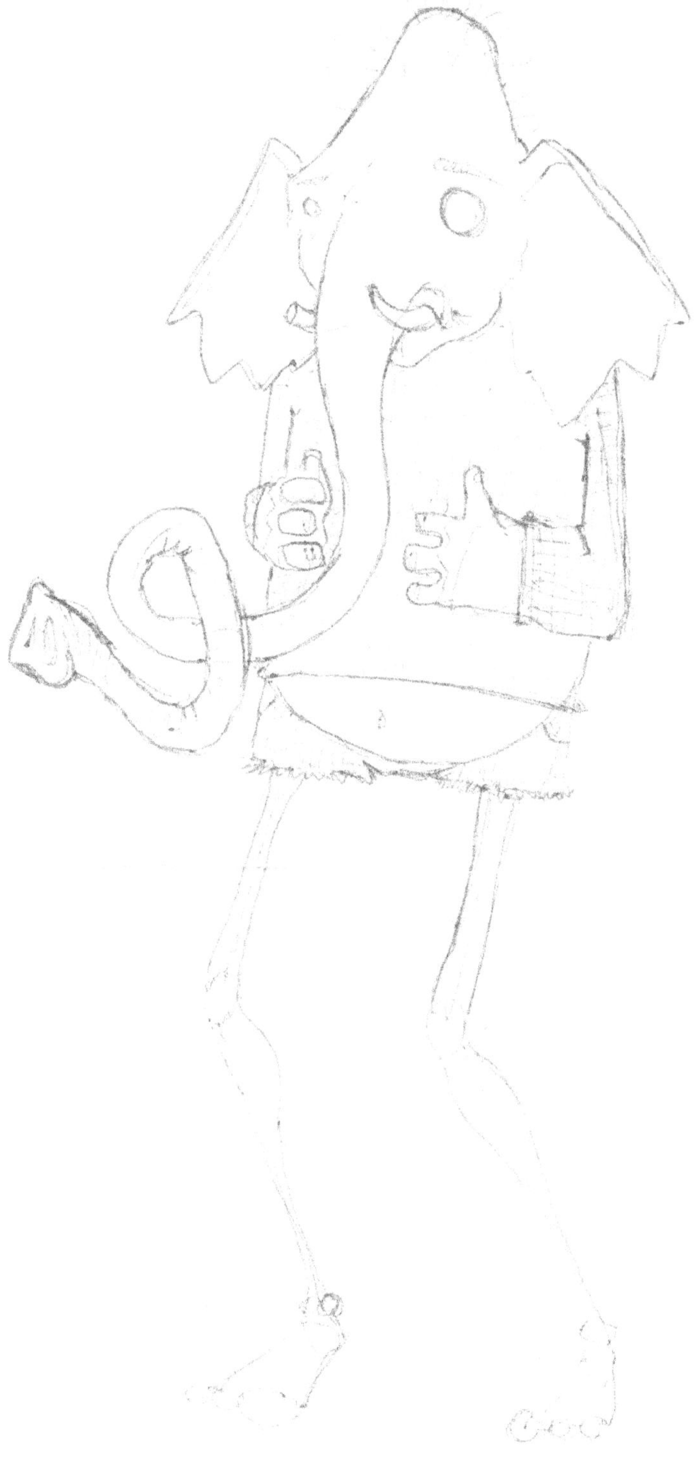

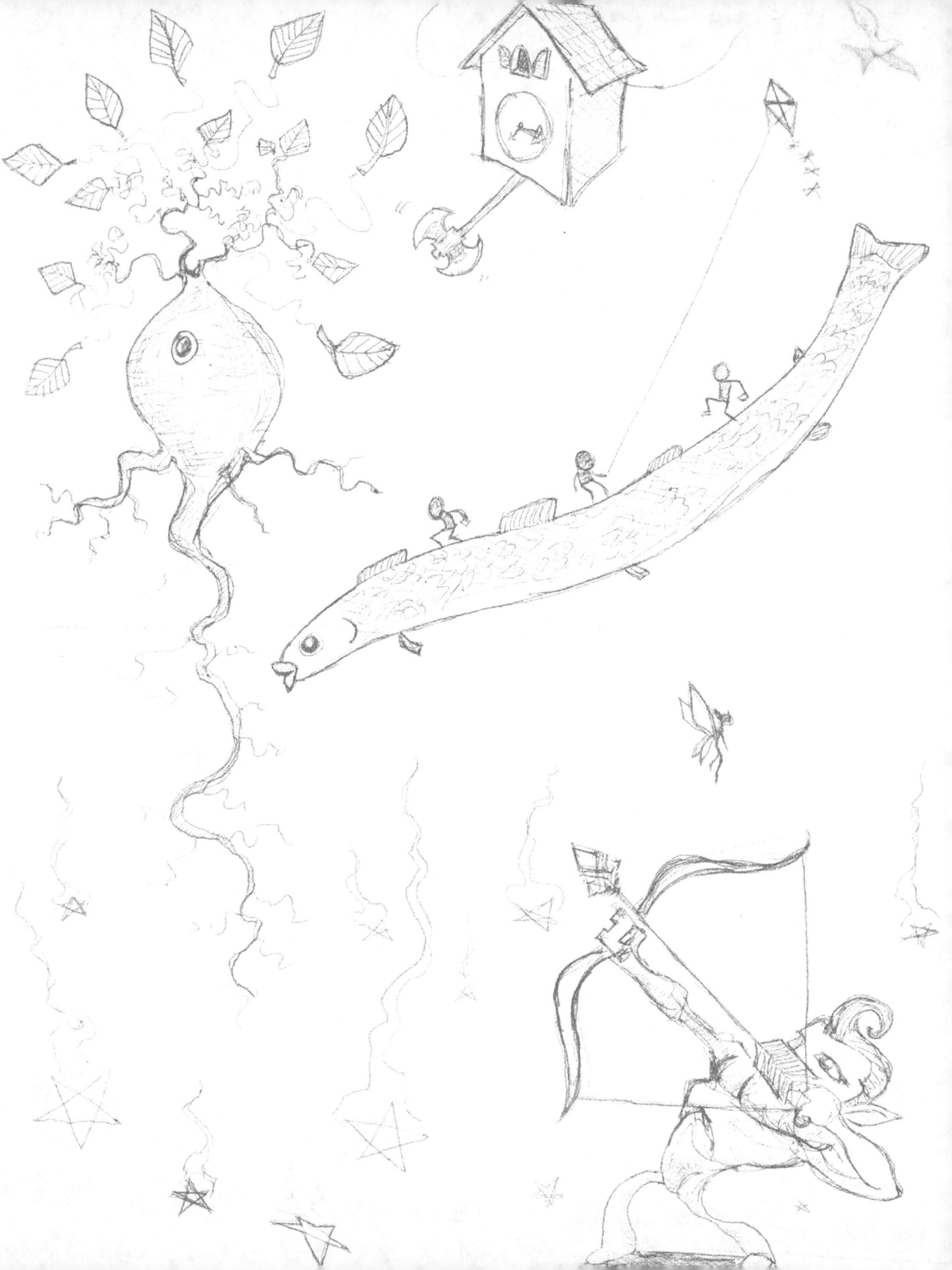

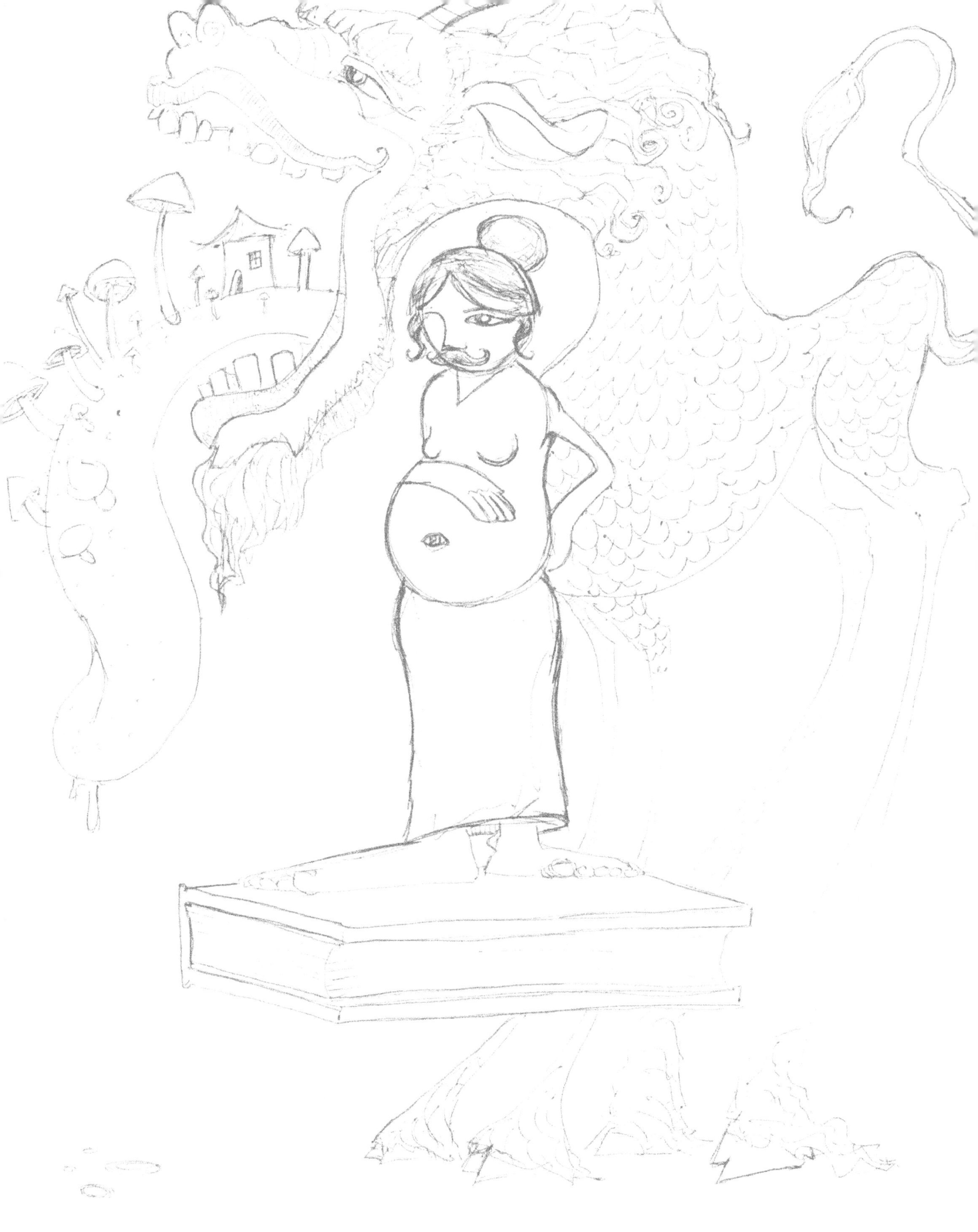

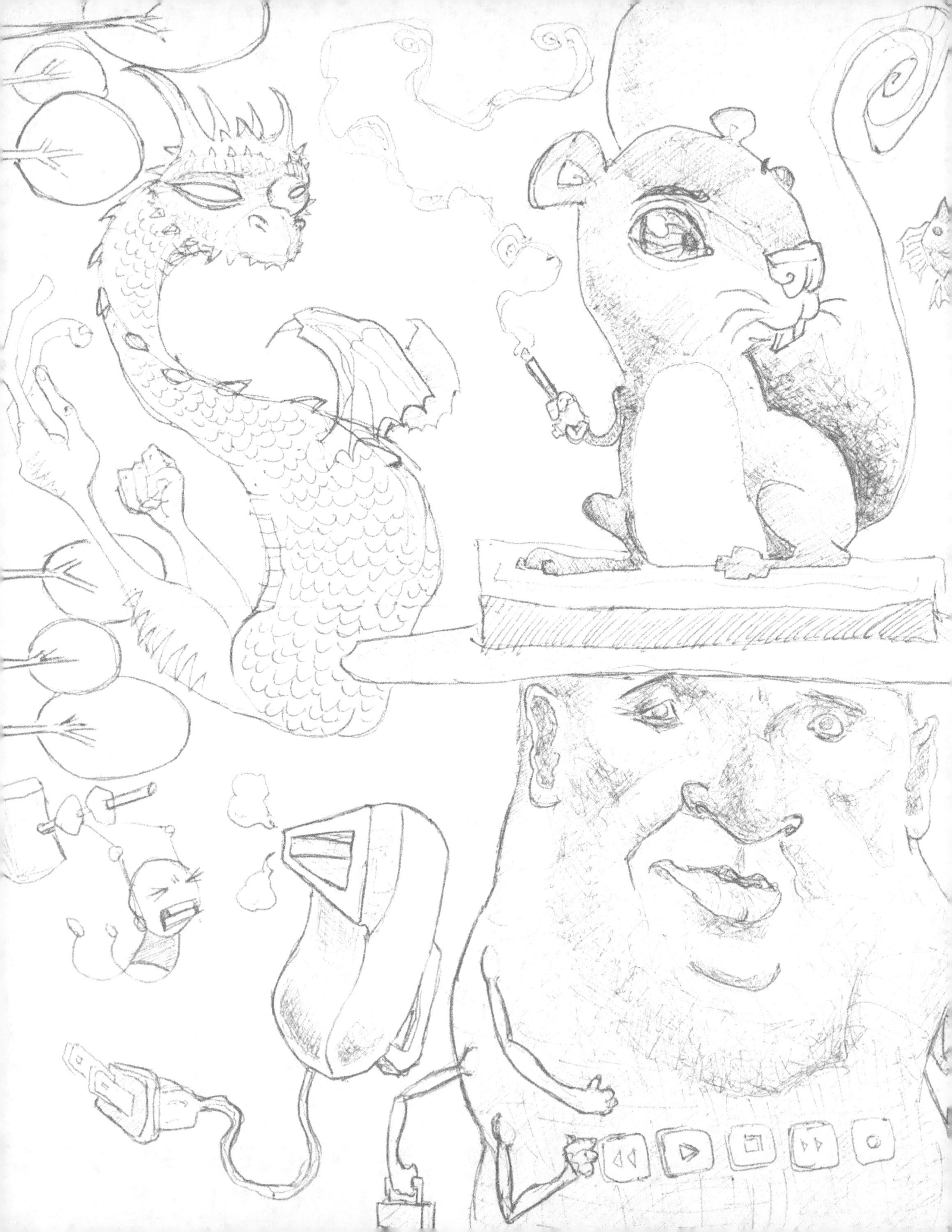

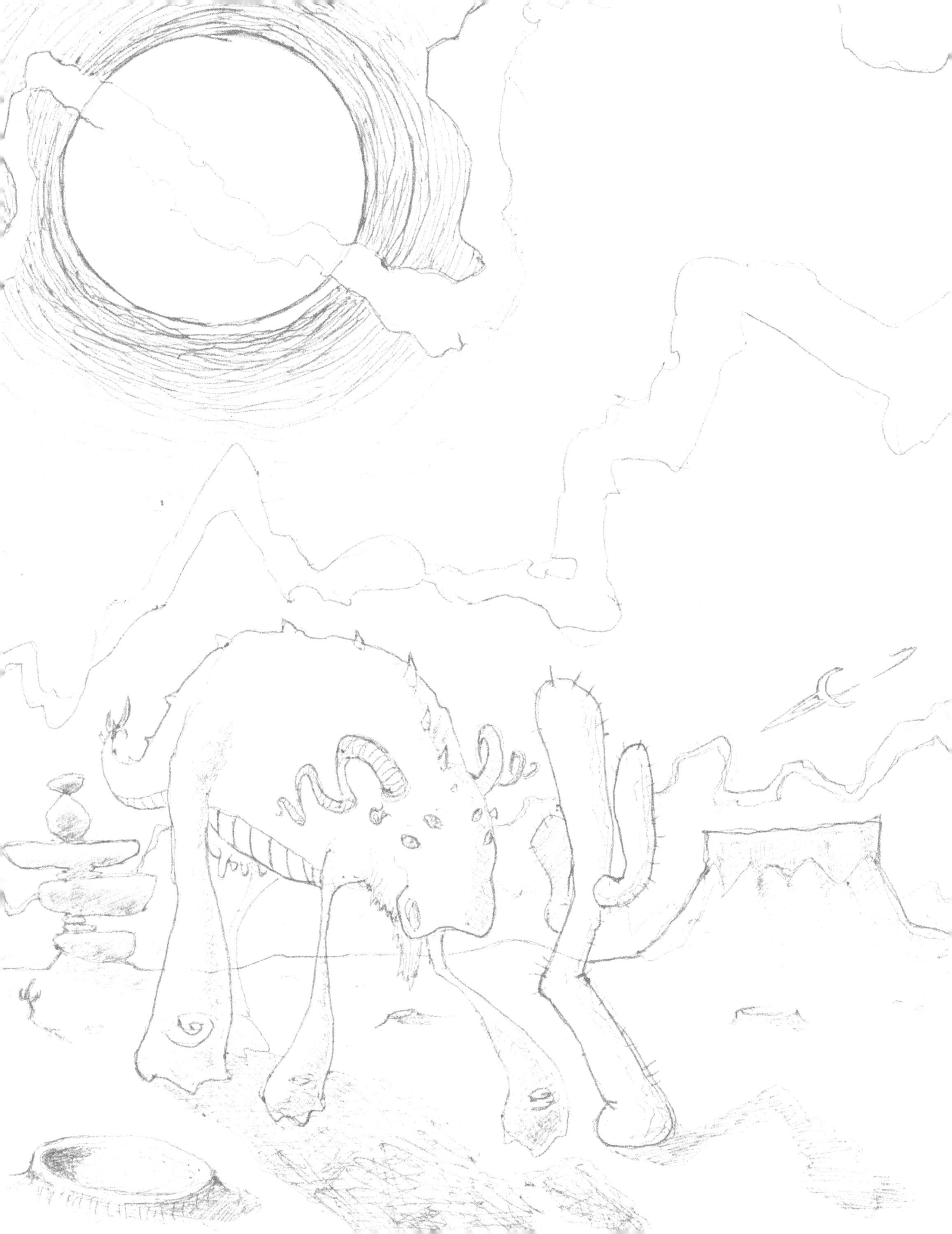

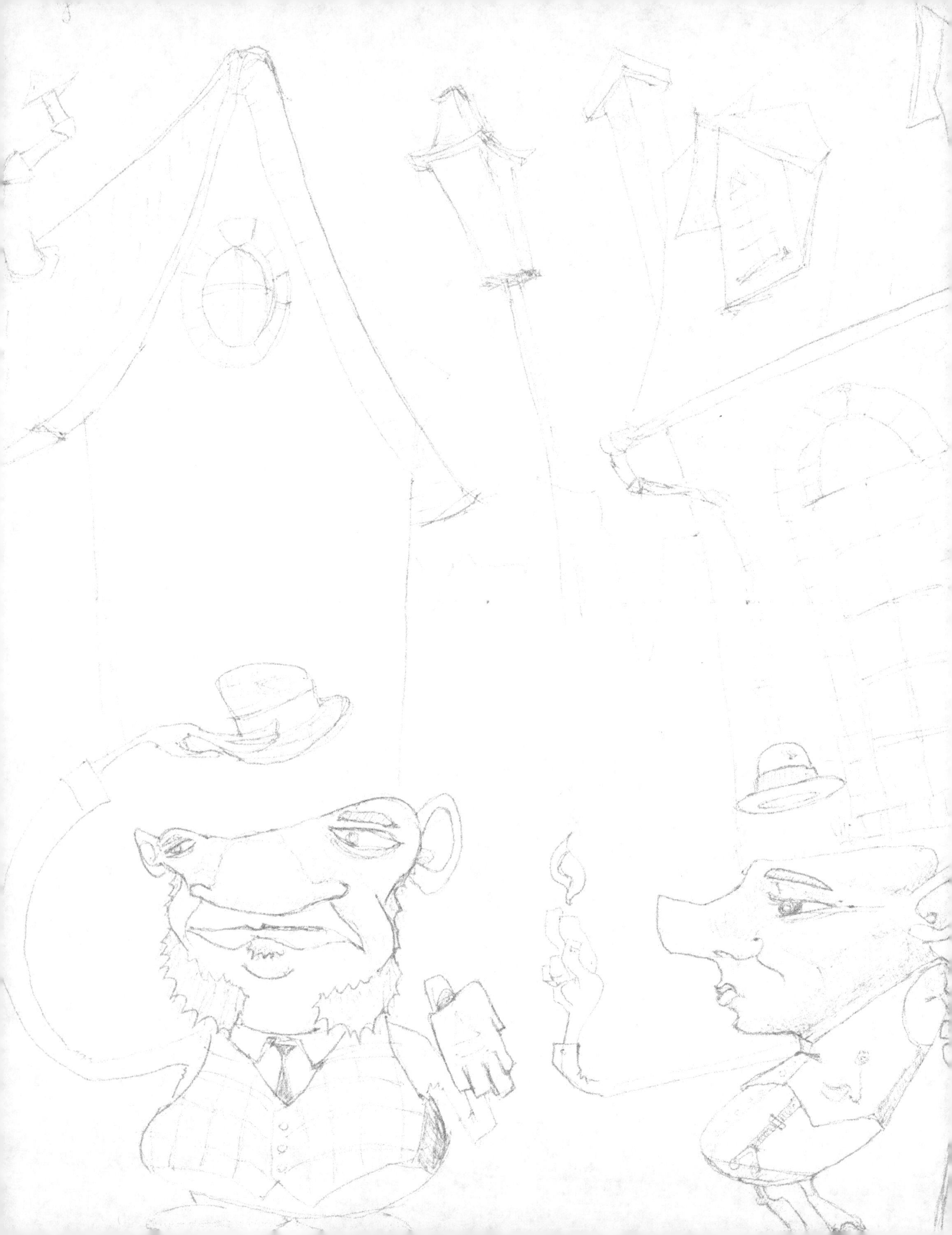

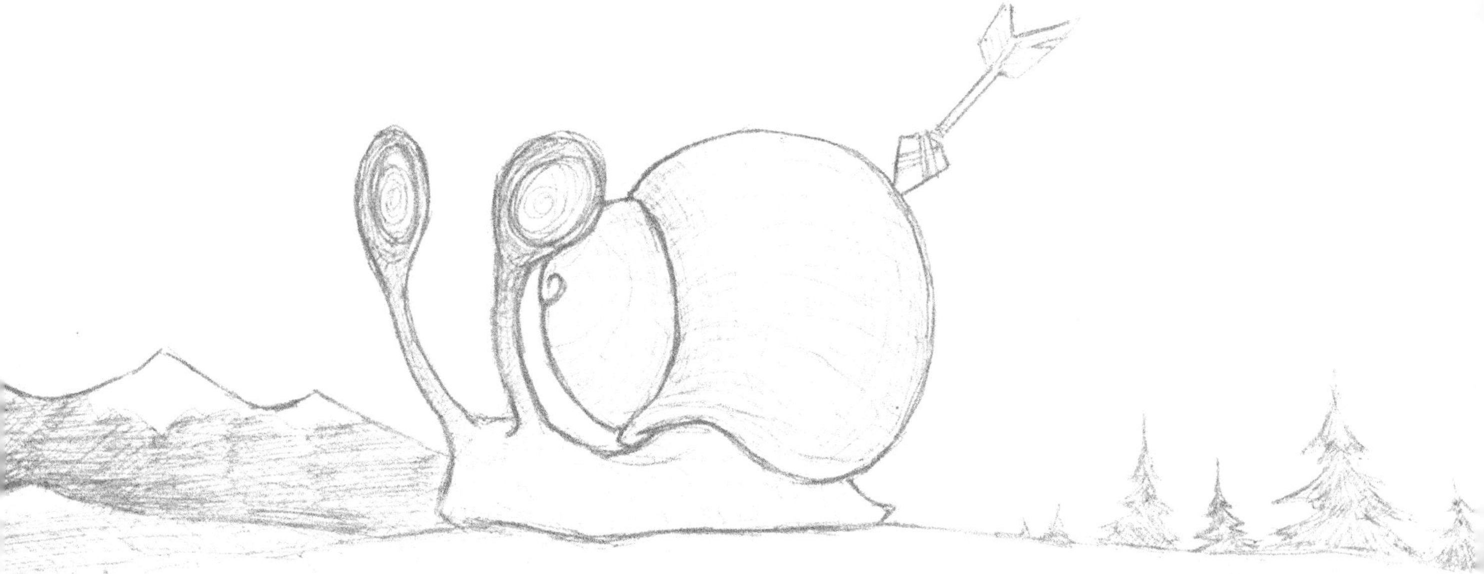

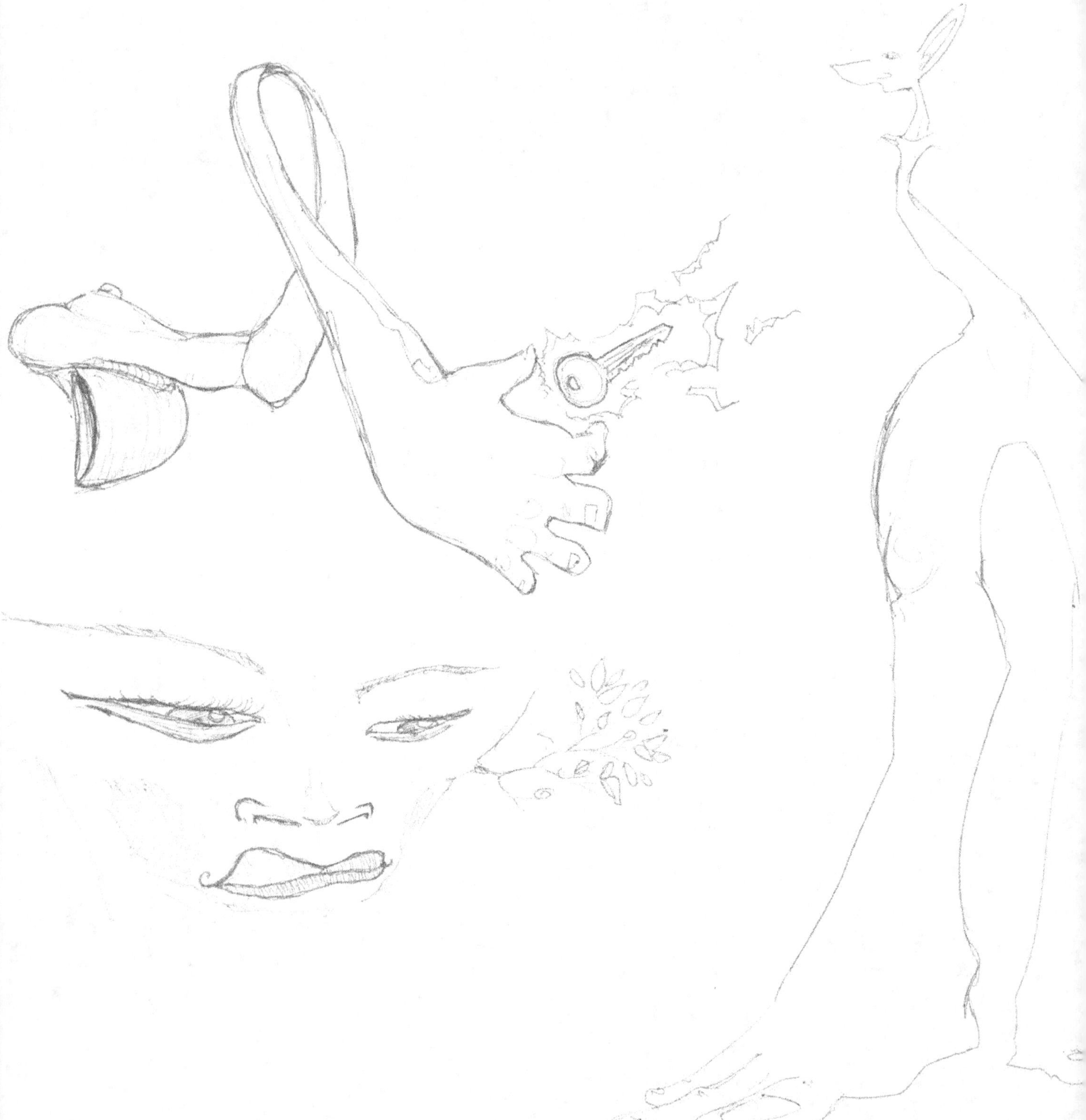

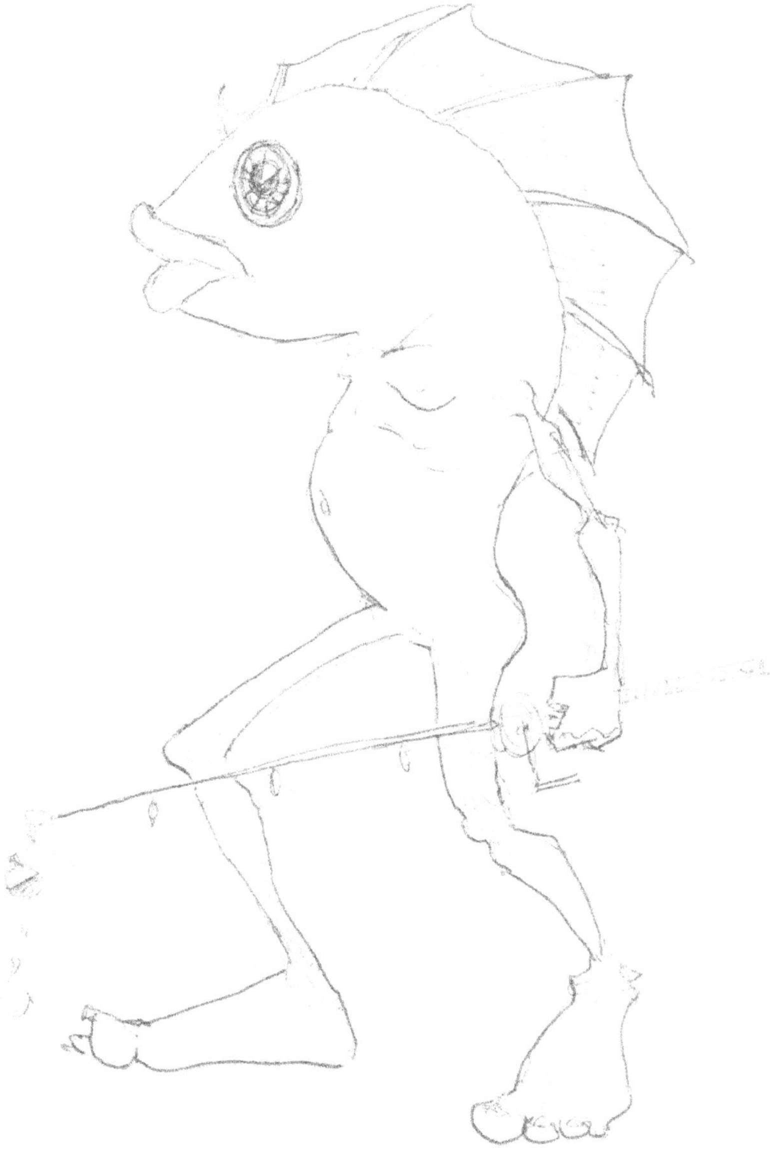

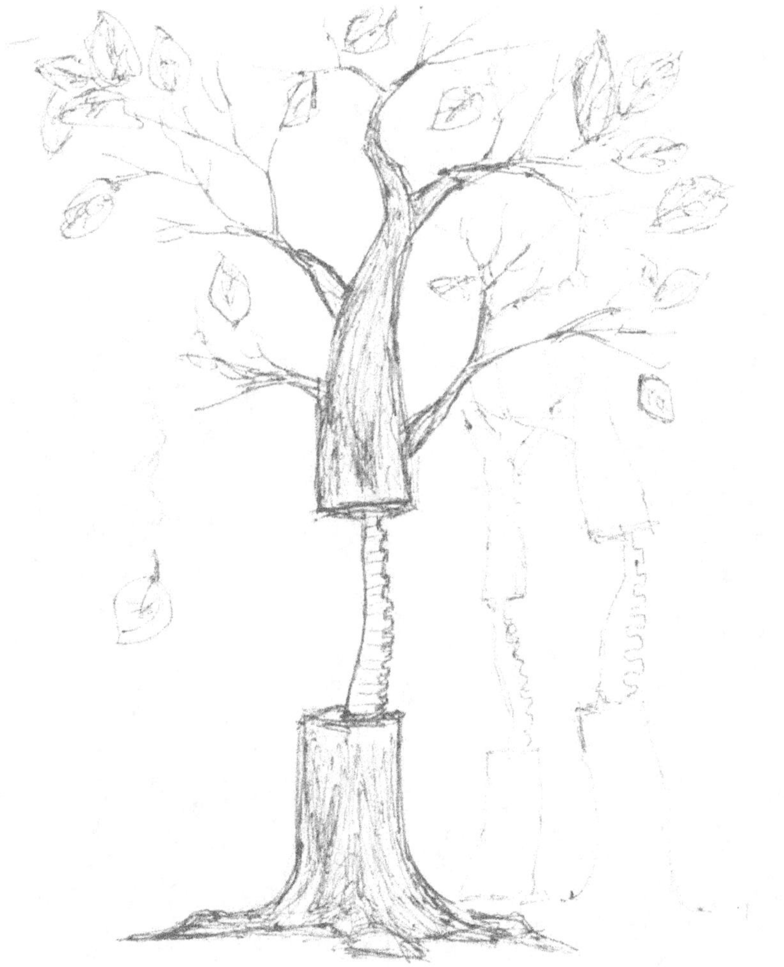

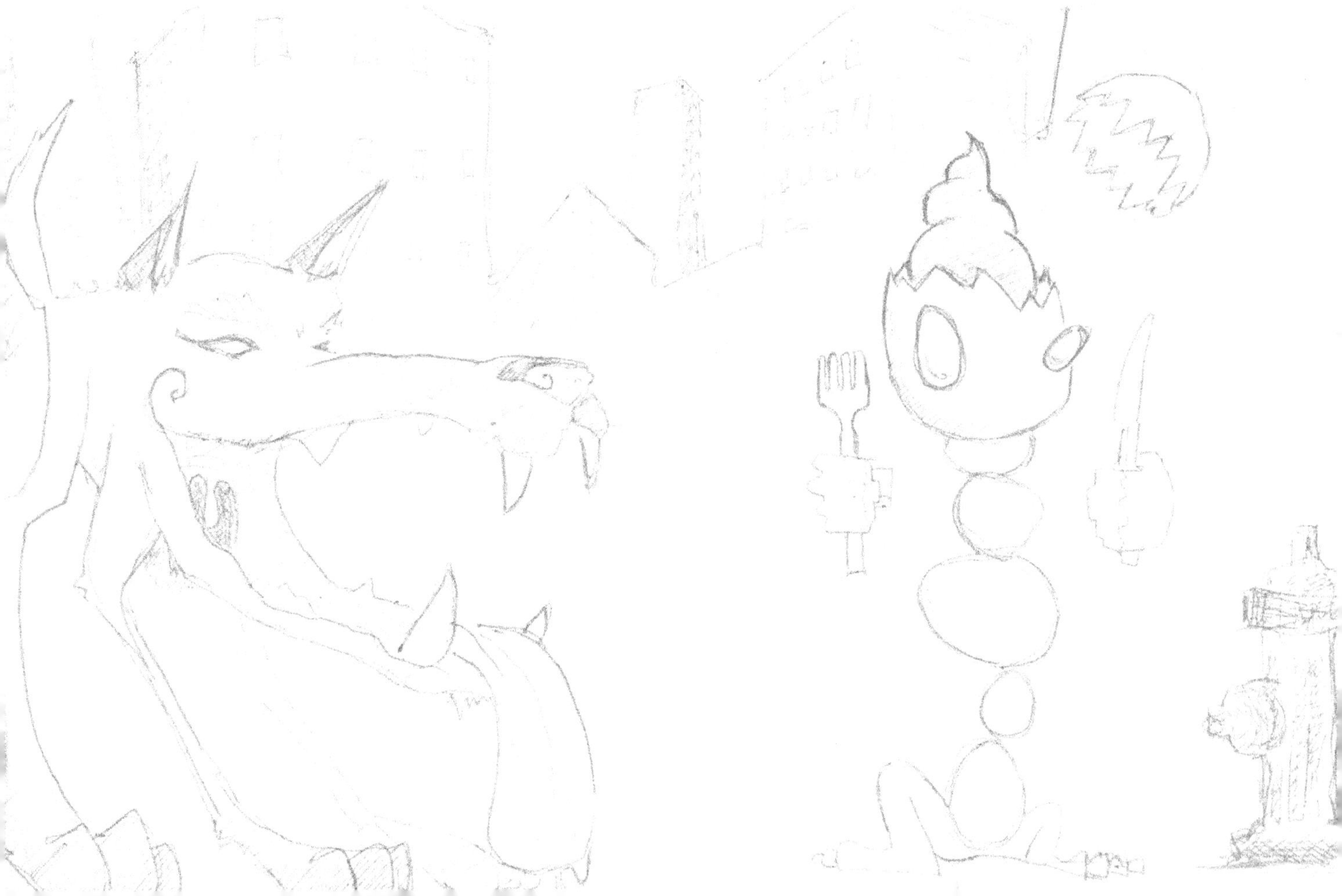

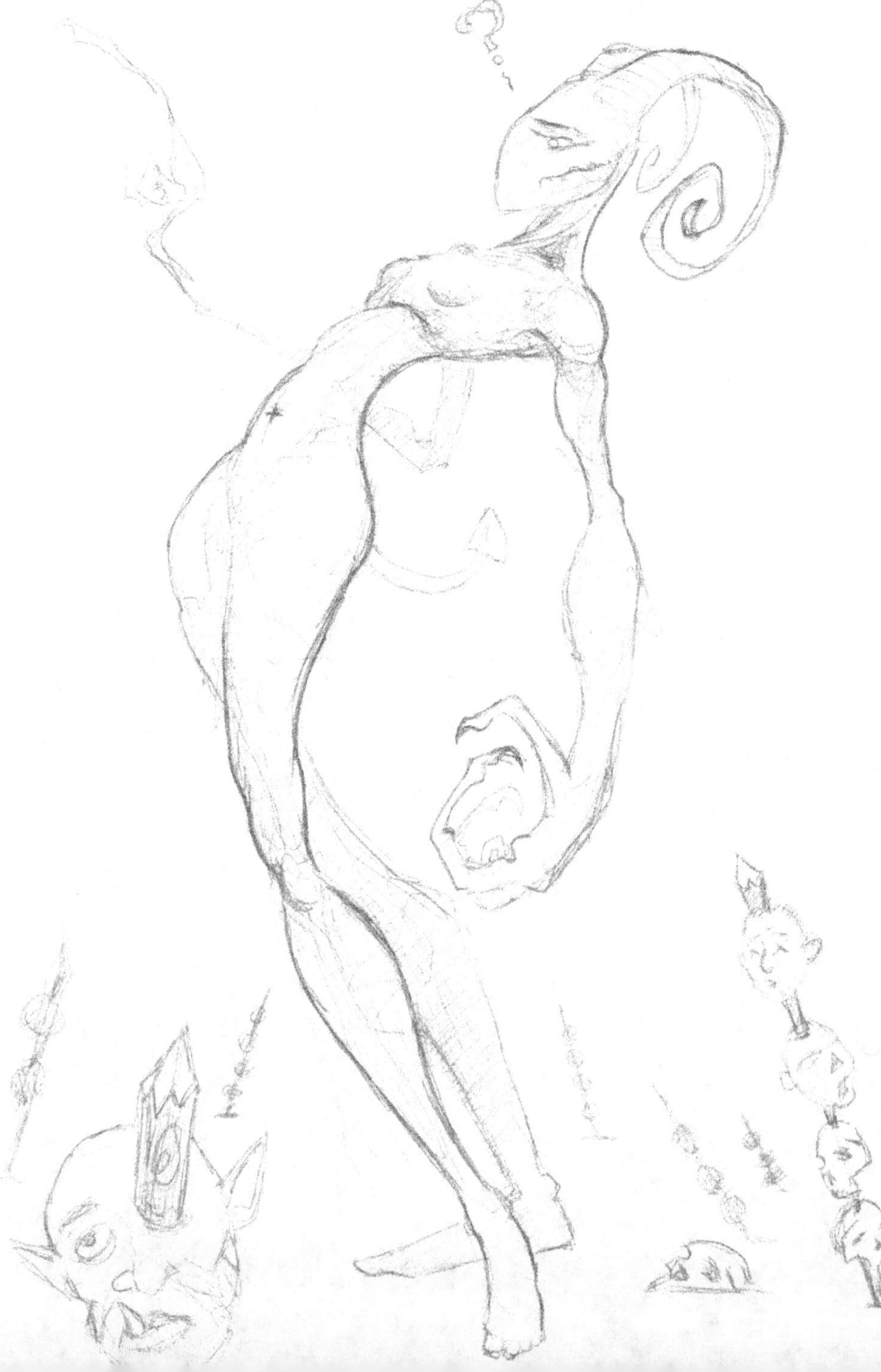

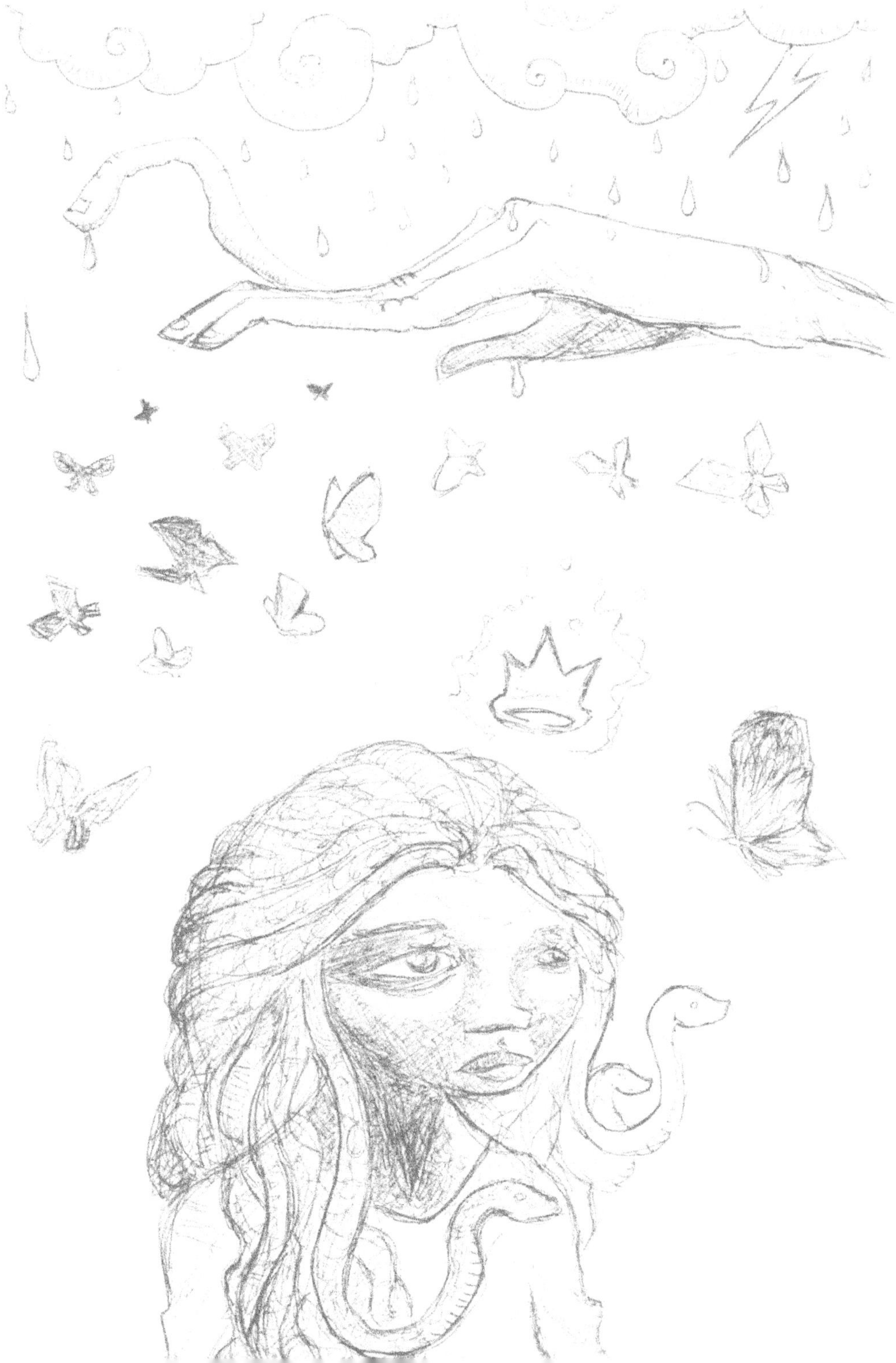

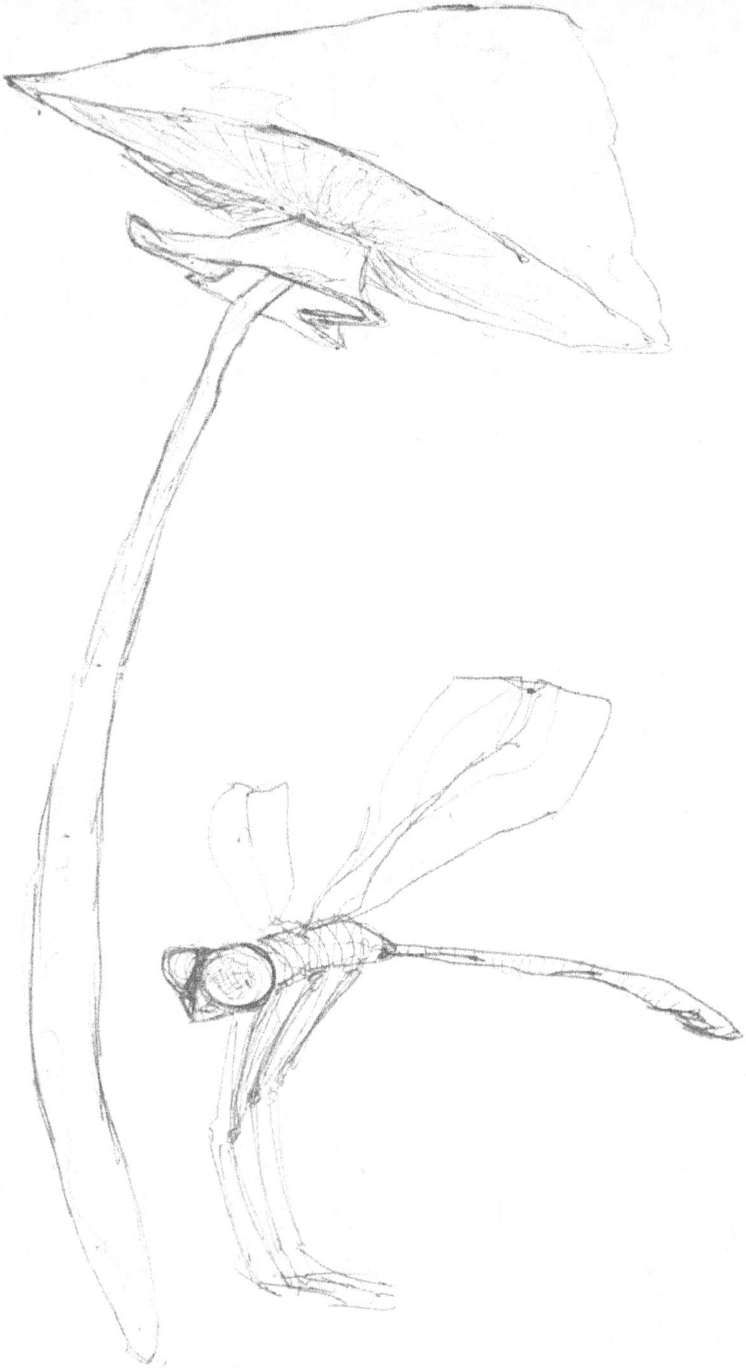

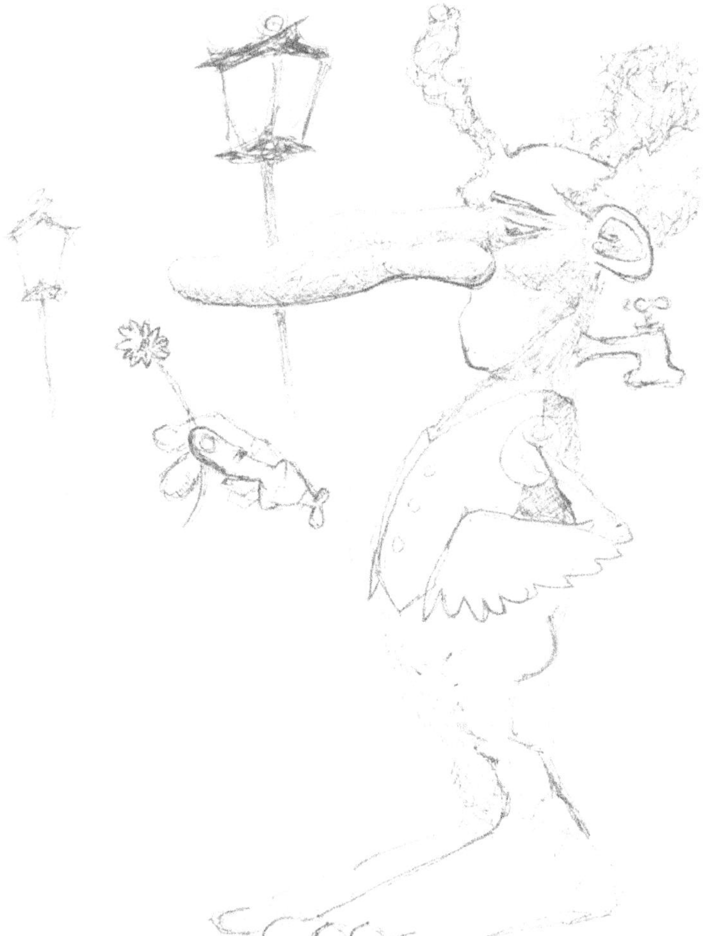

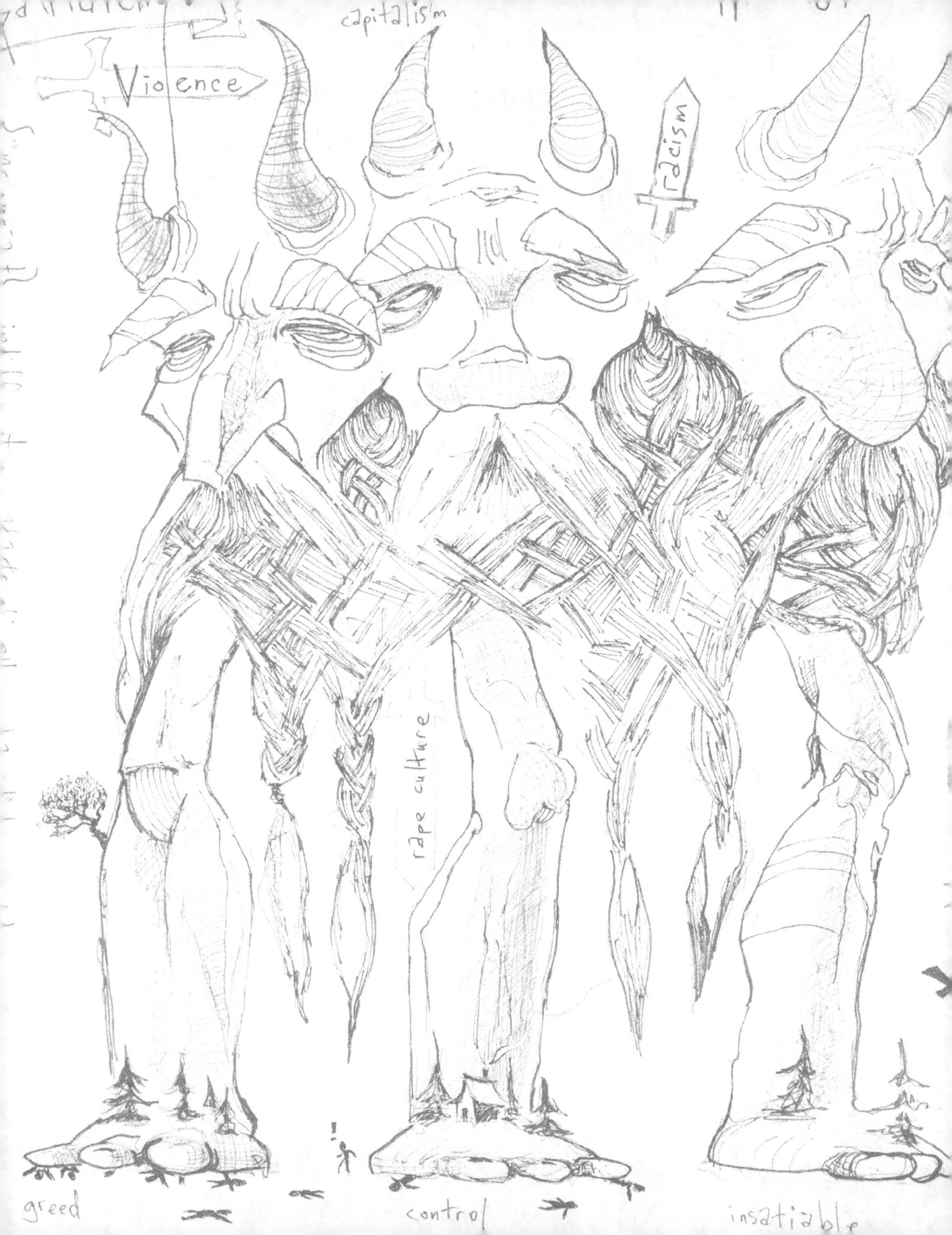
capitalism
Violence
racism
rape culture
greed
control
insatiable

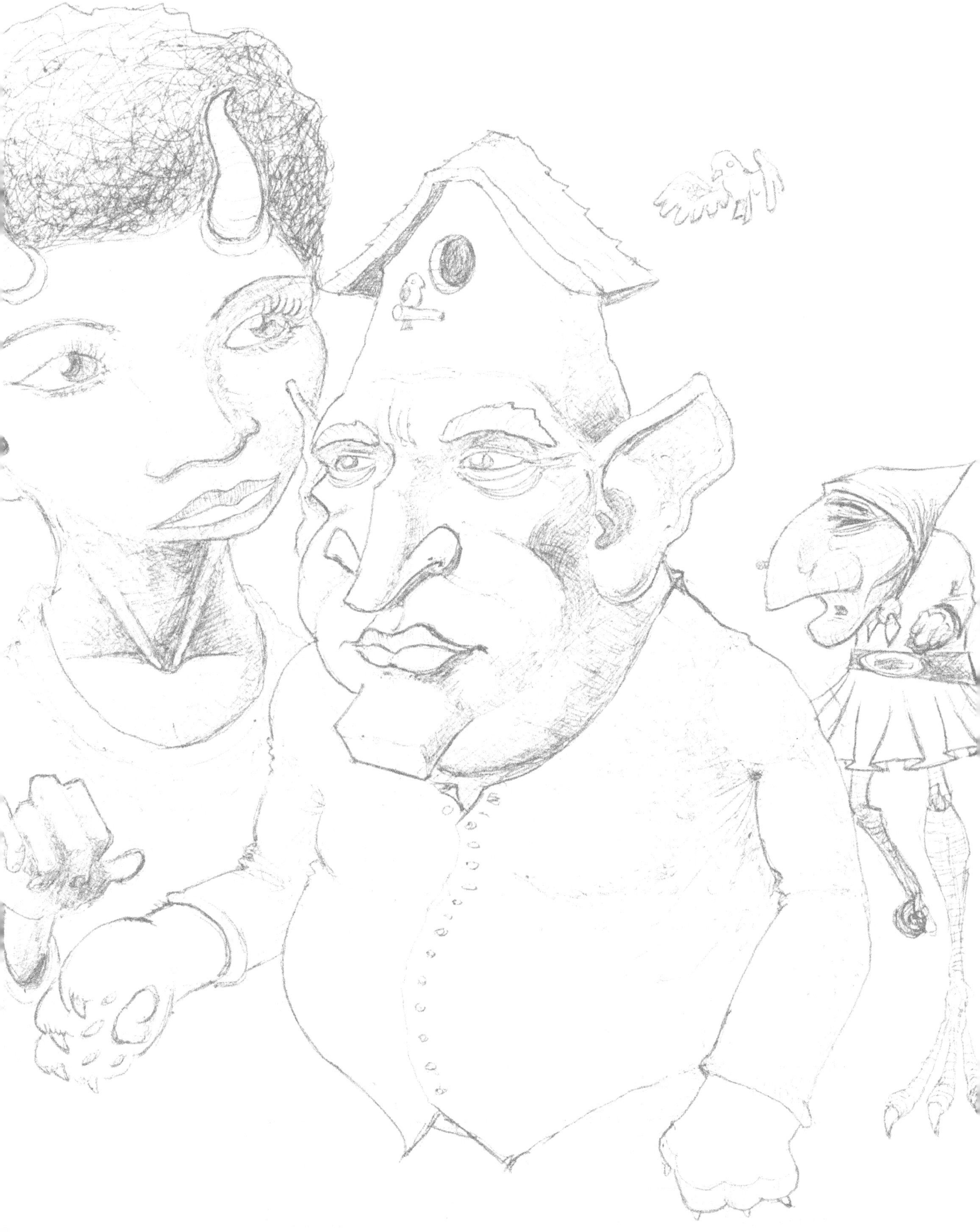

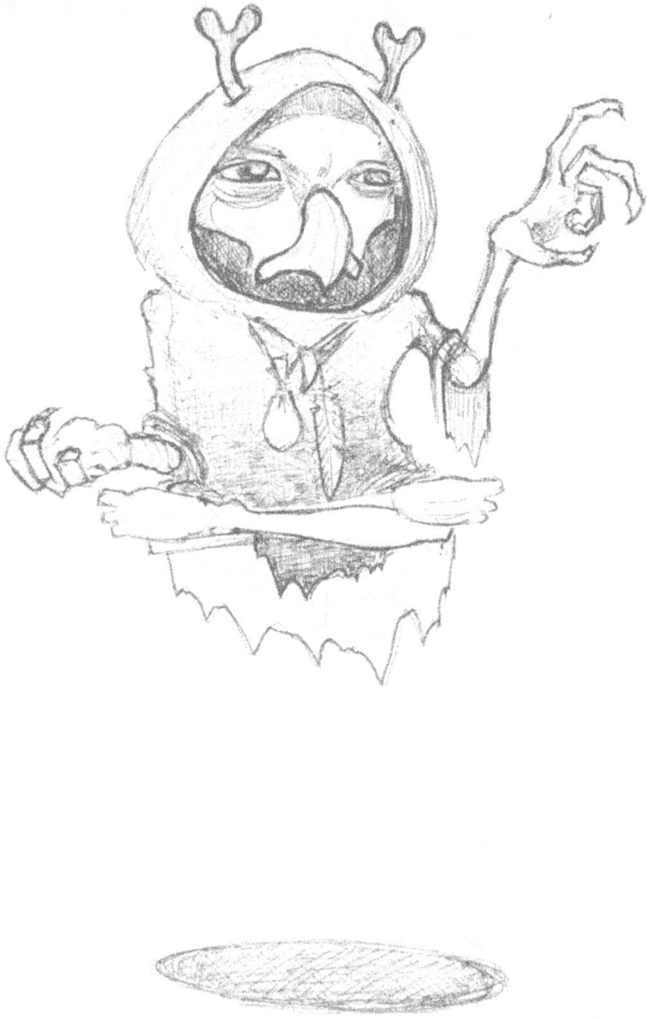

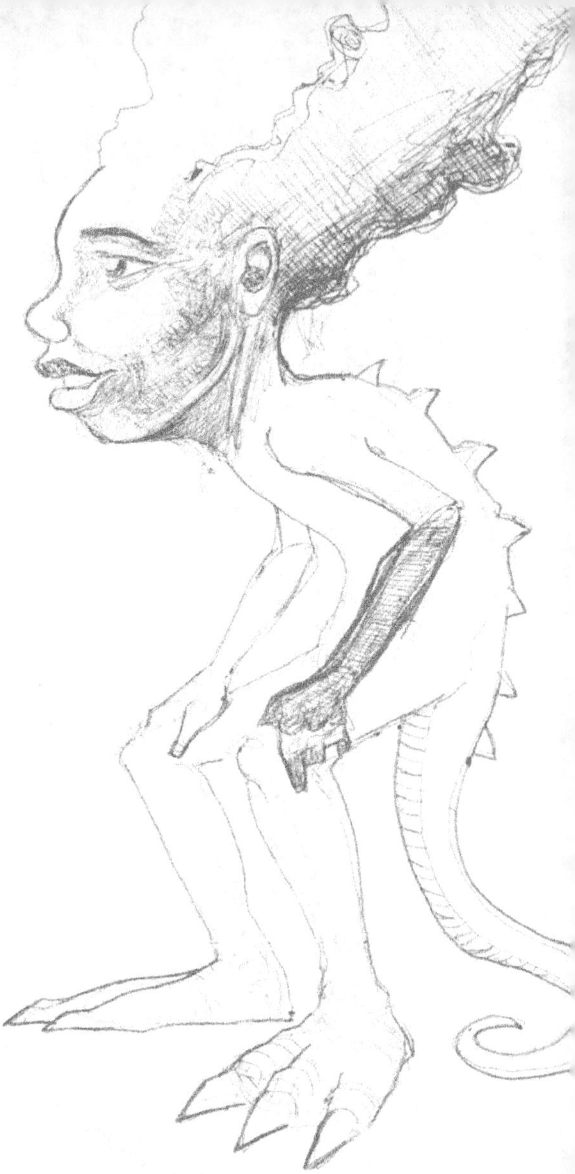

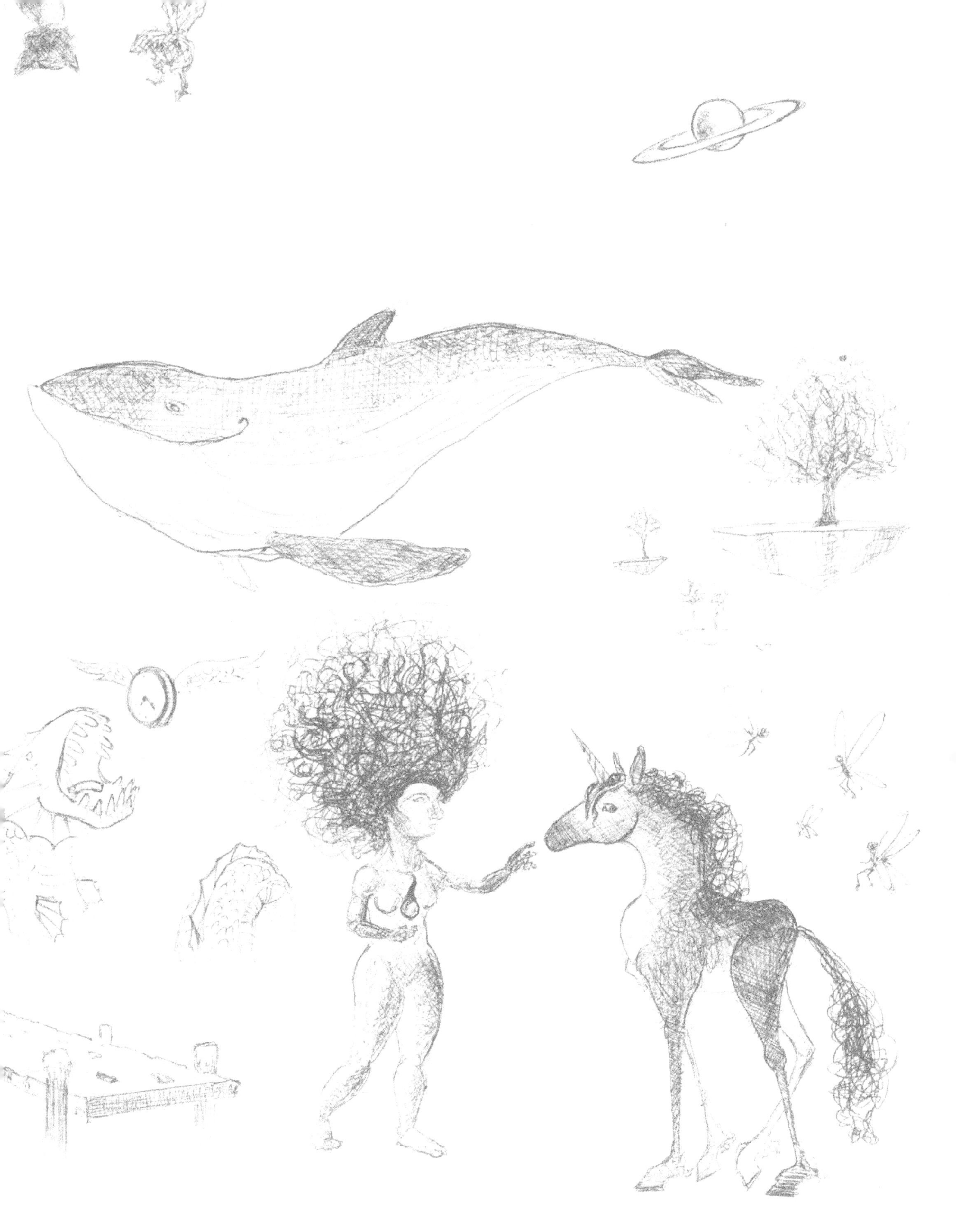

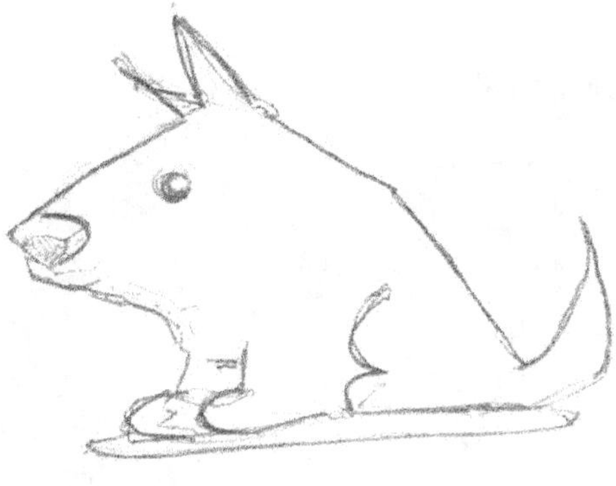

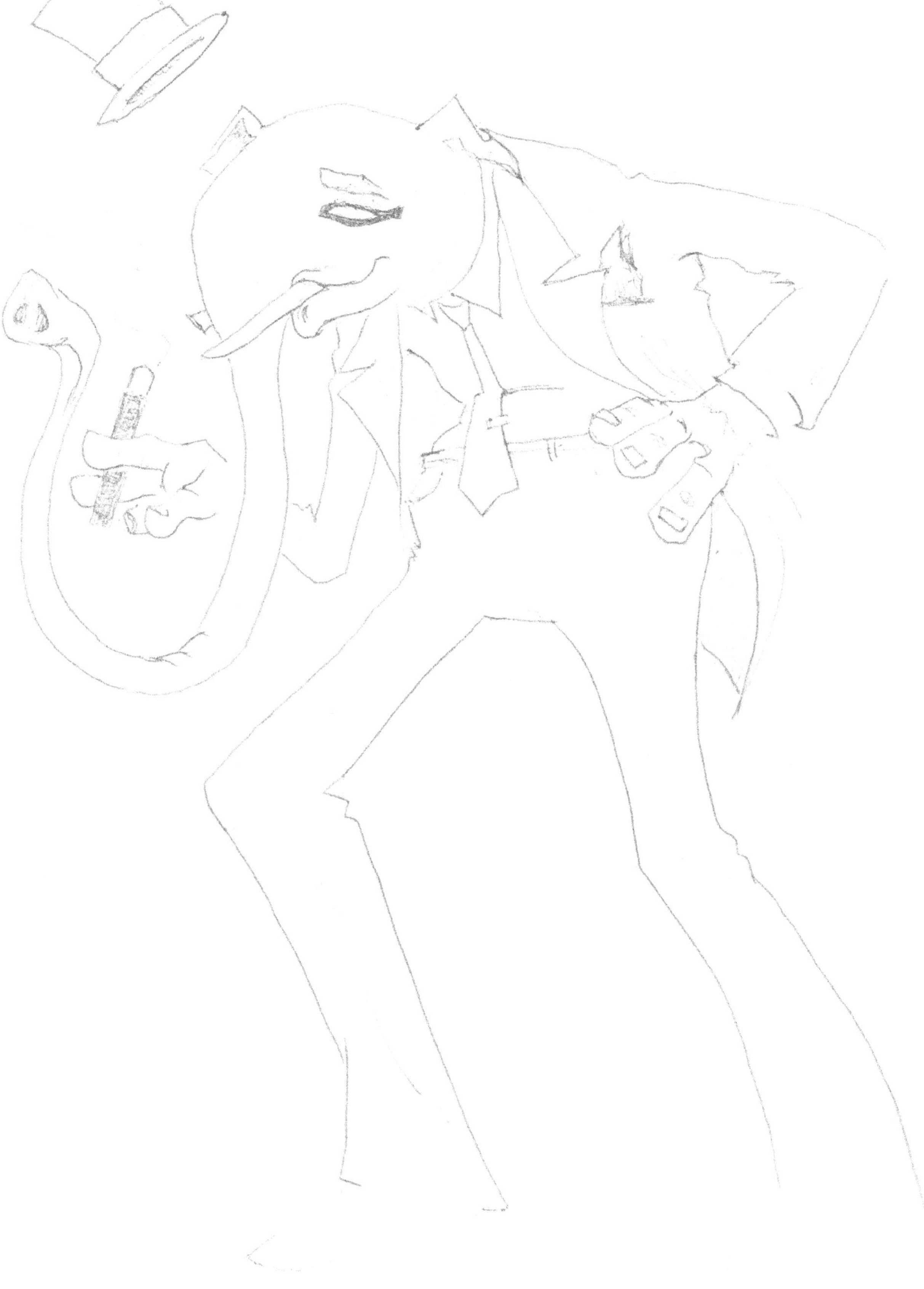

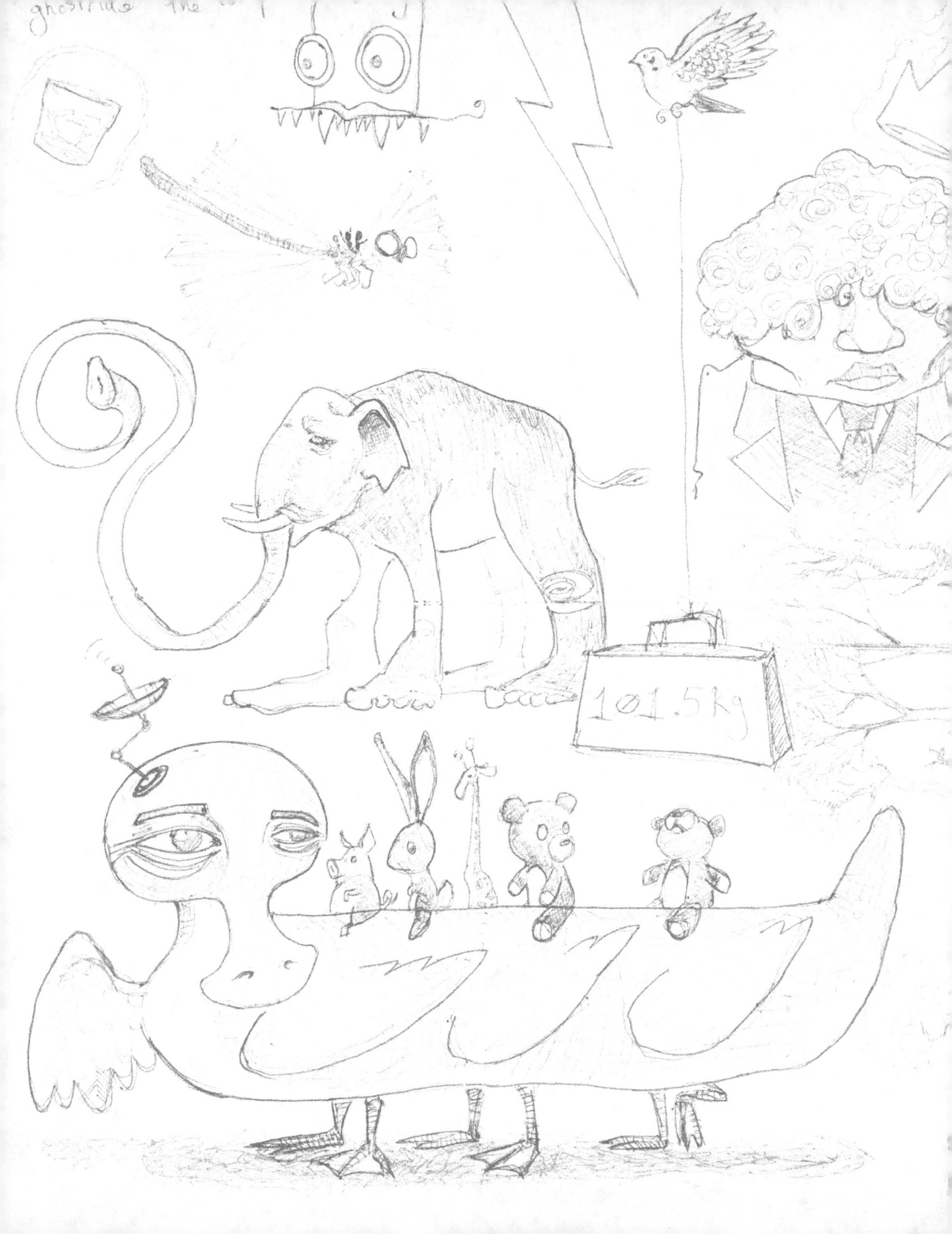
101.5kg

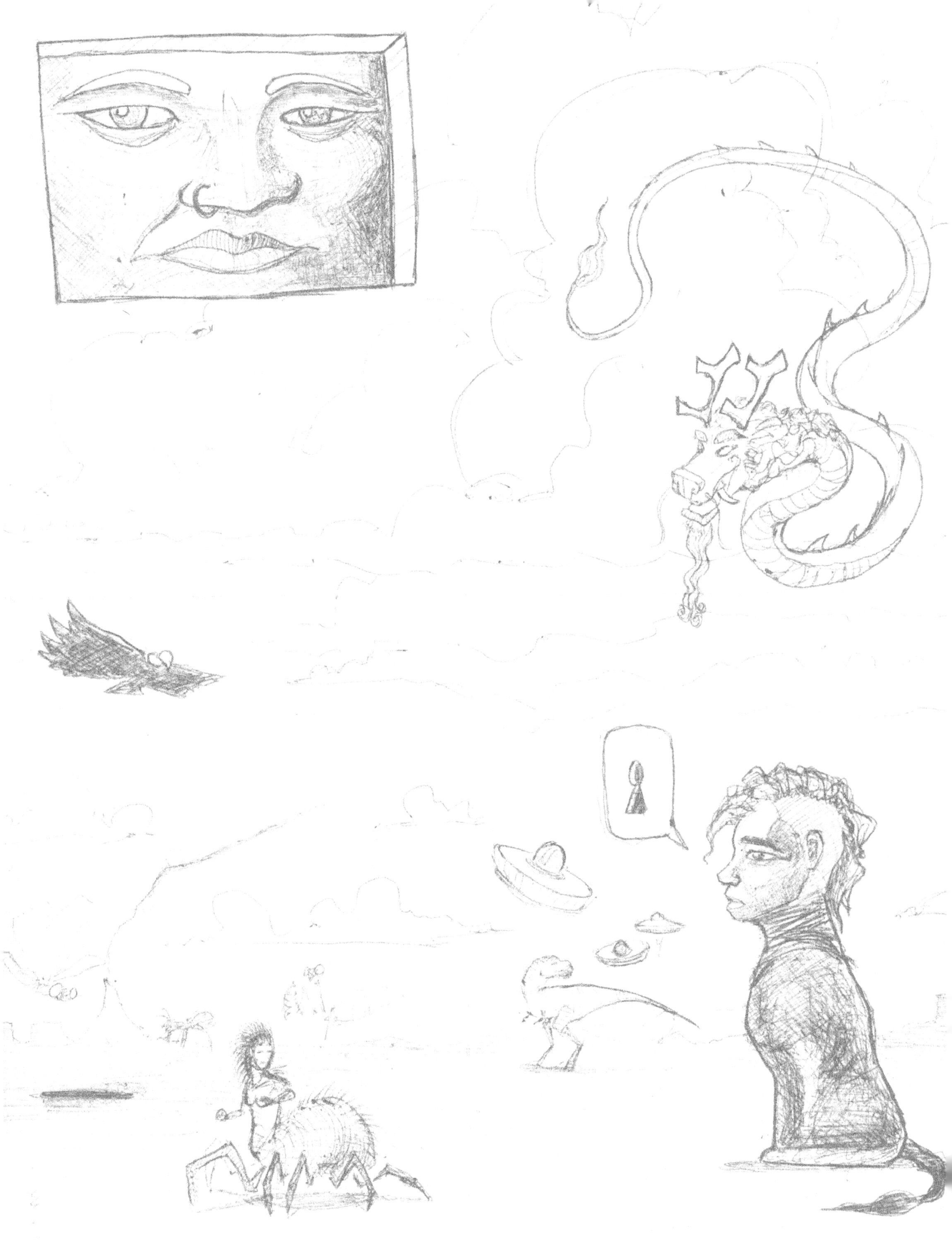

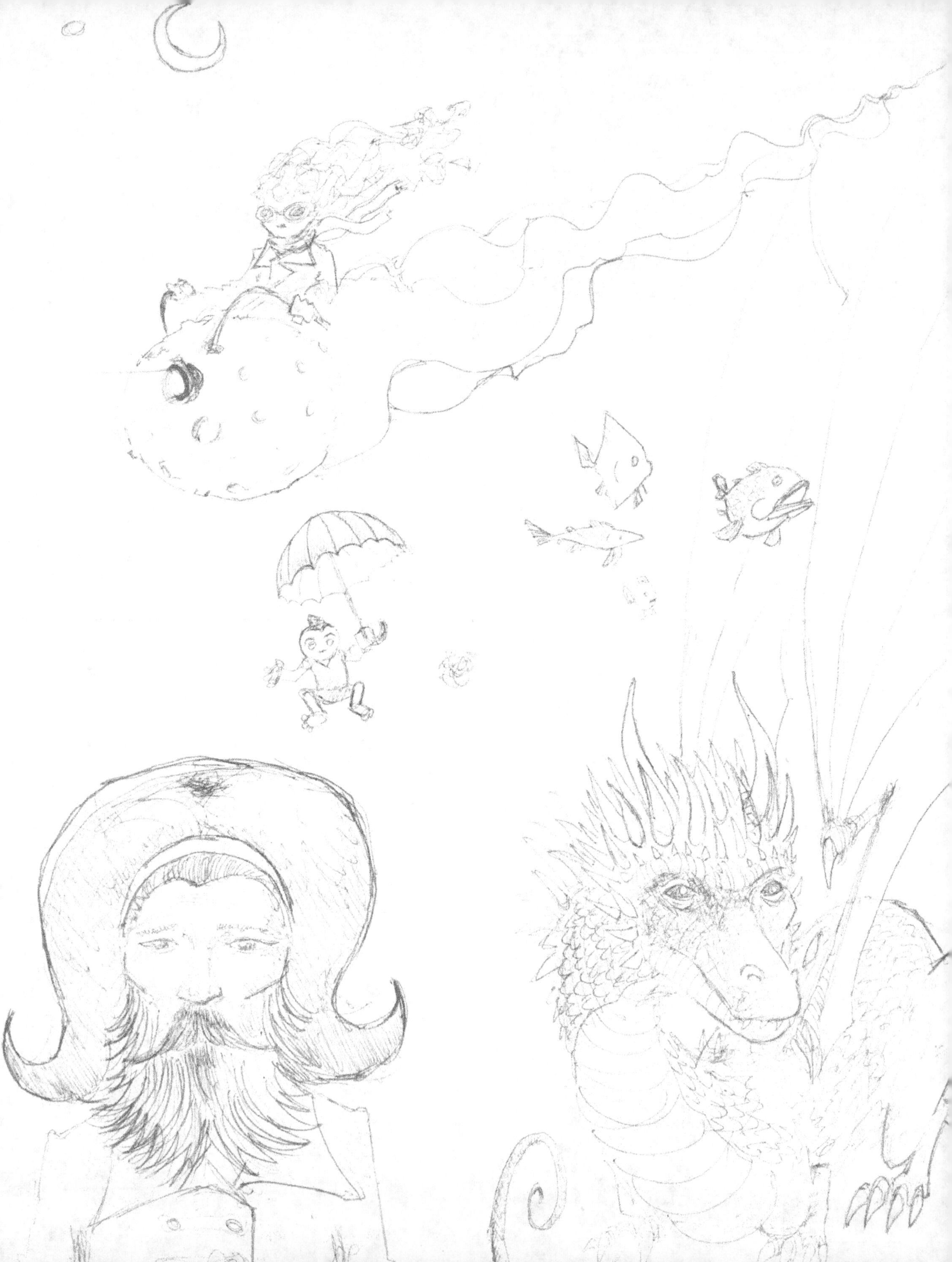

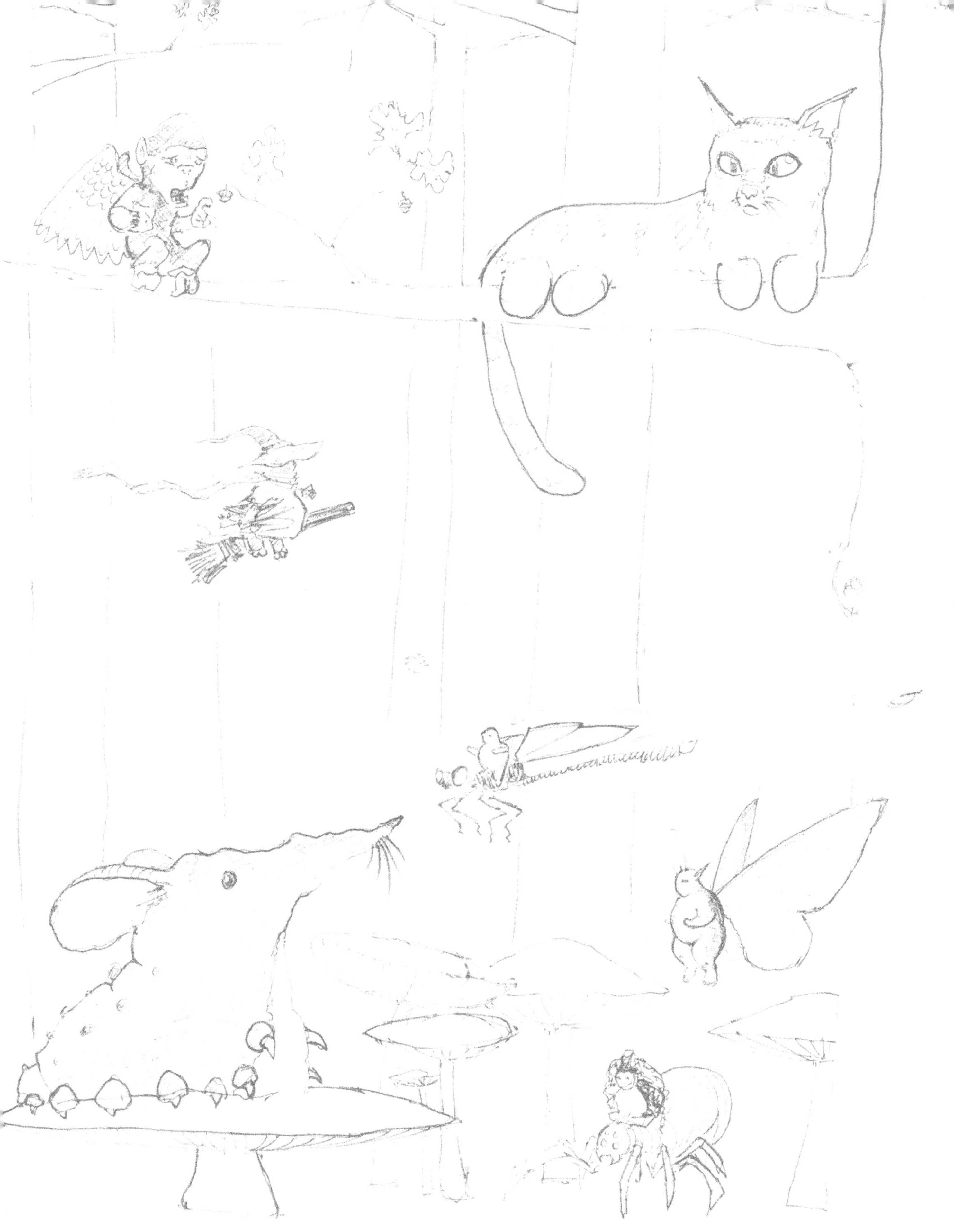

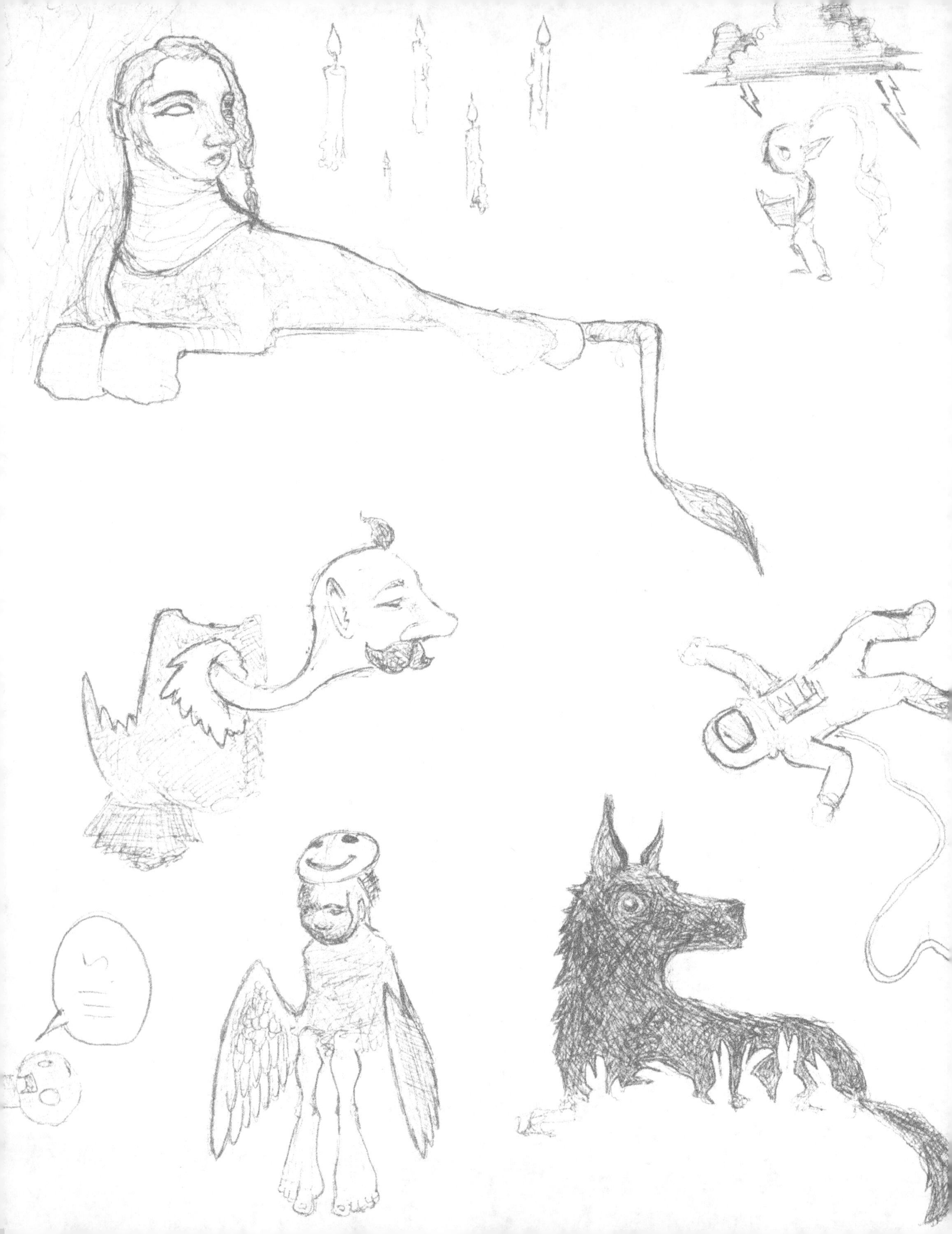

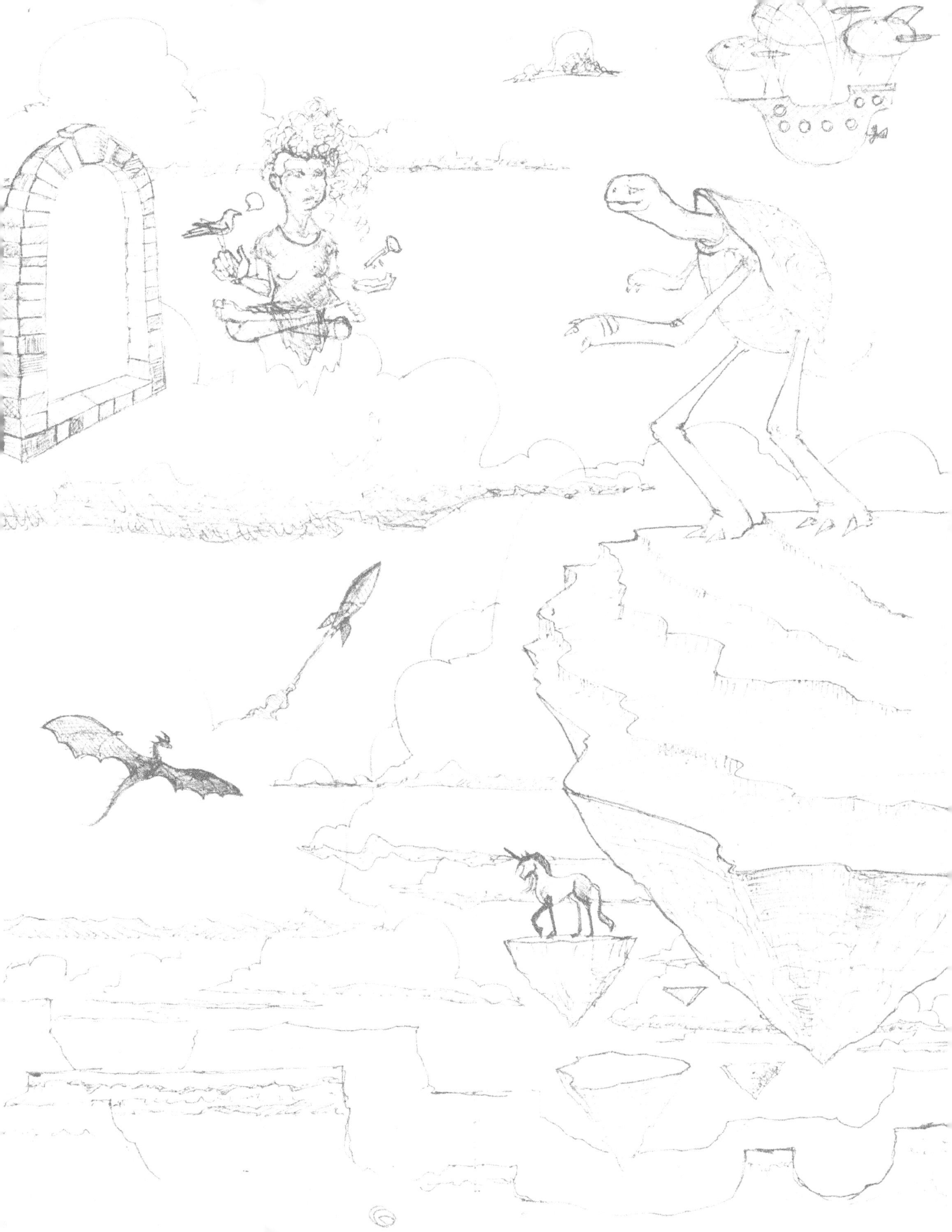

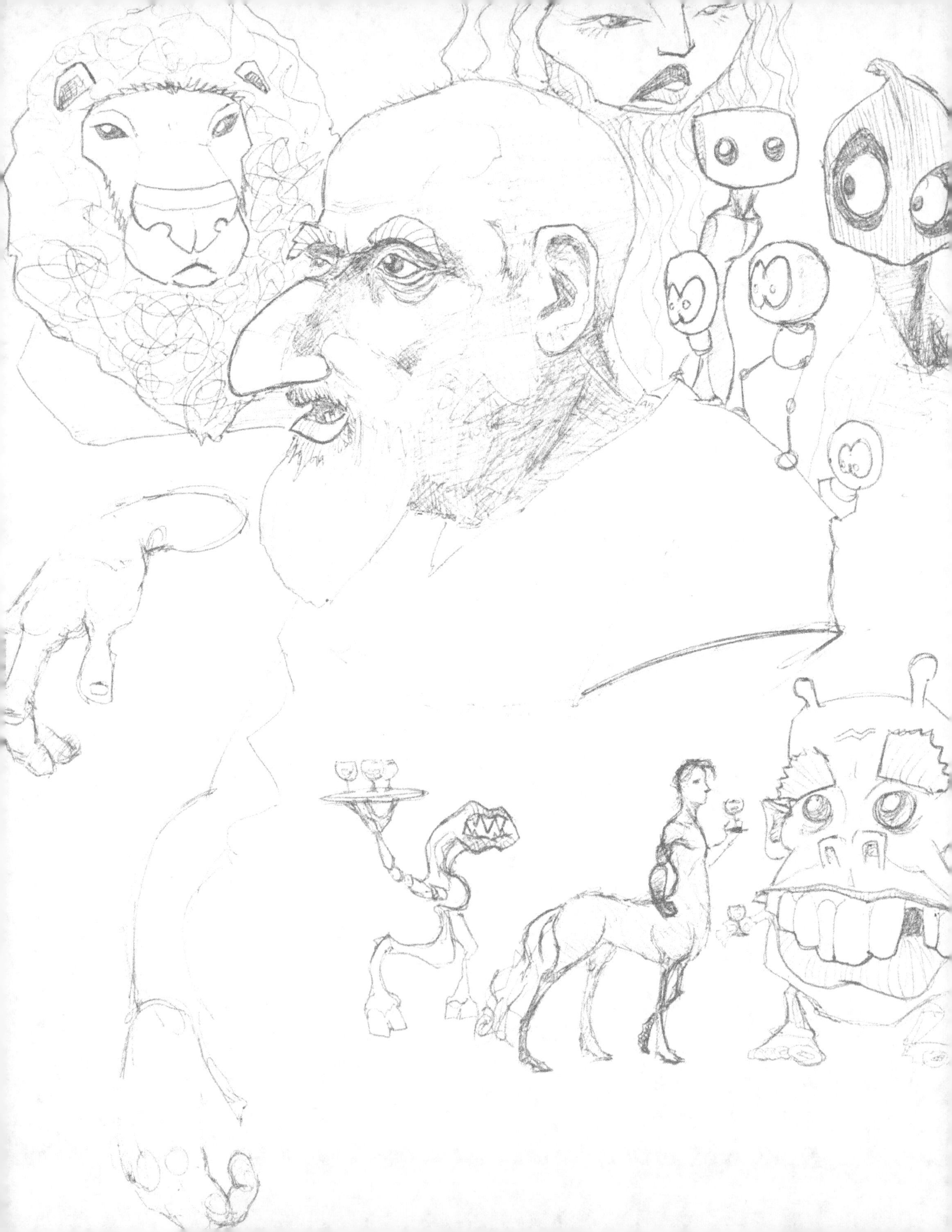

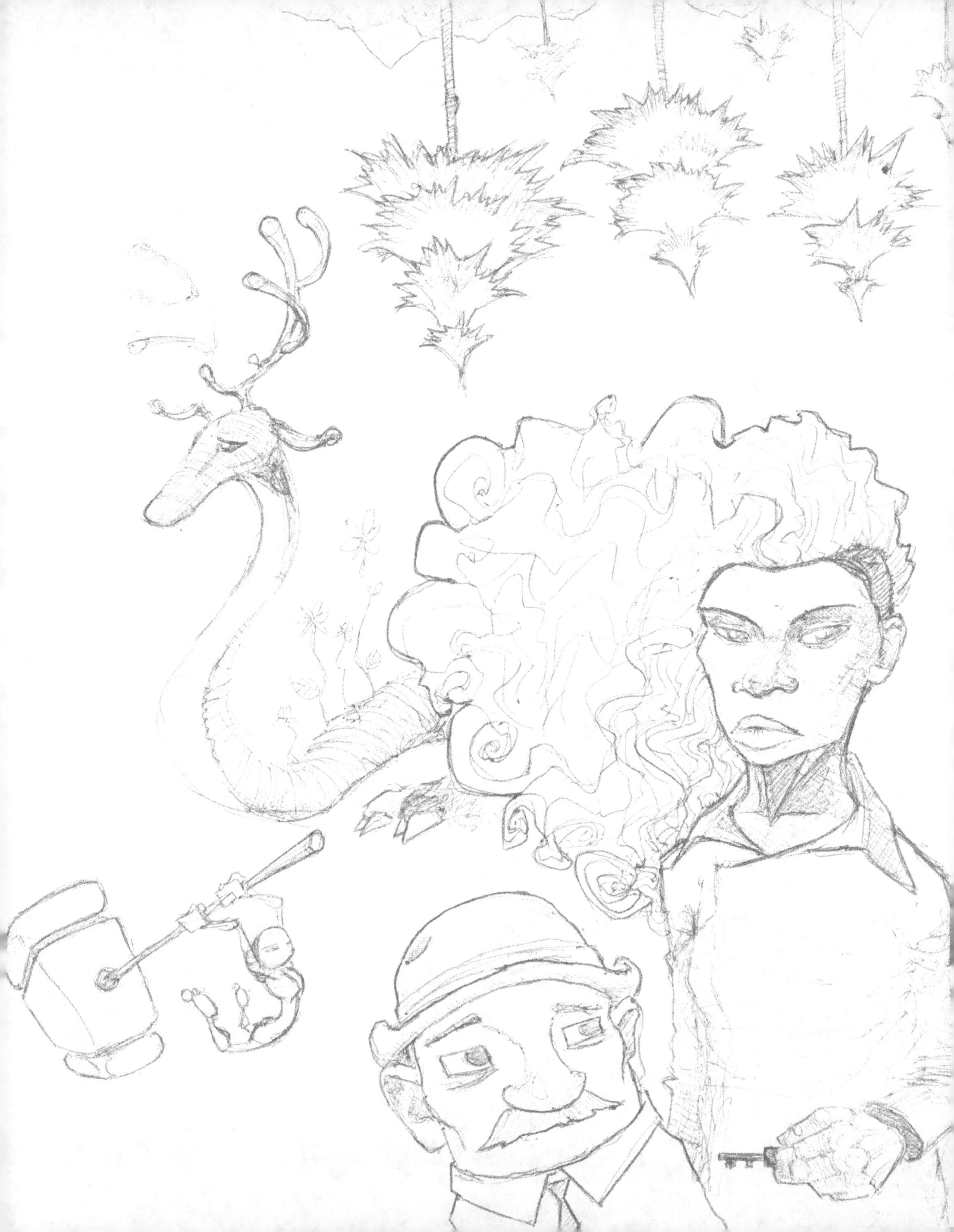

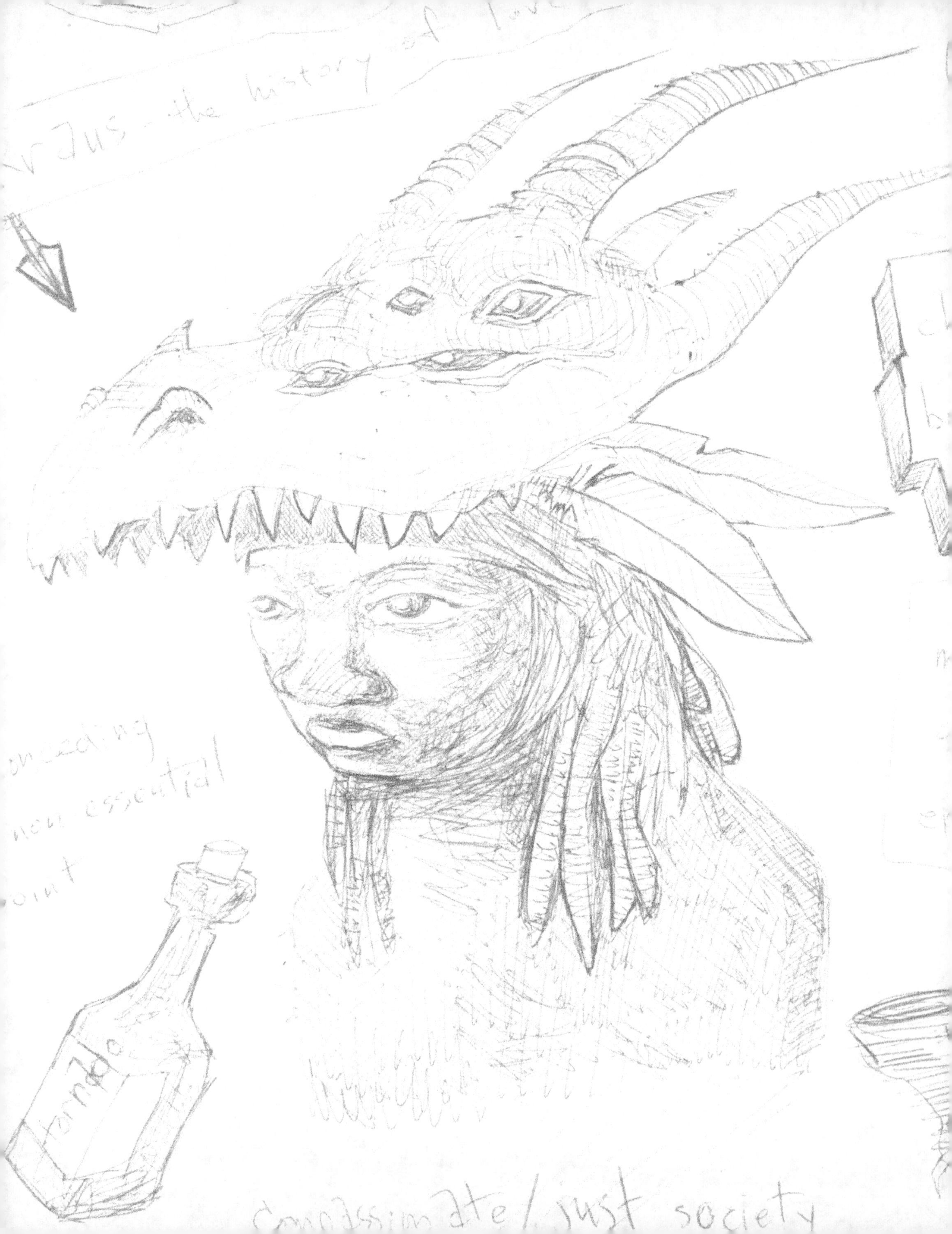
the history of
conceding
non essential
compassimate/ just society

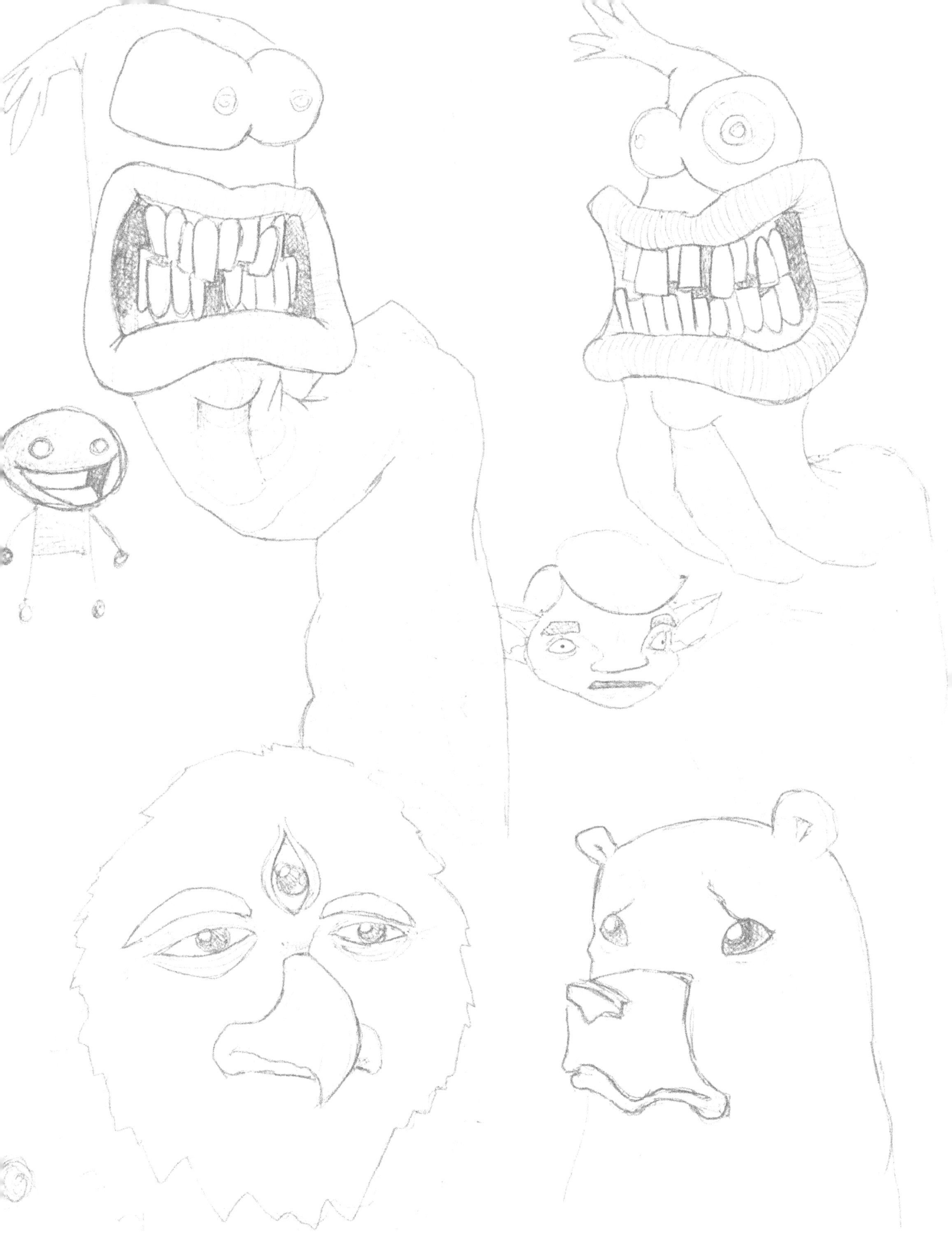

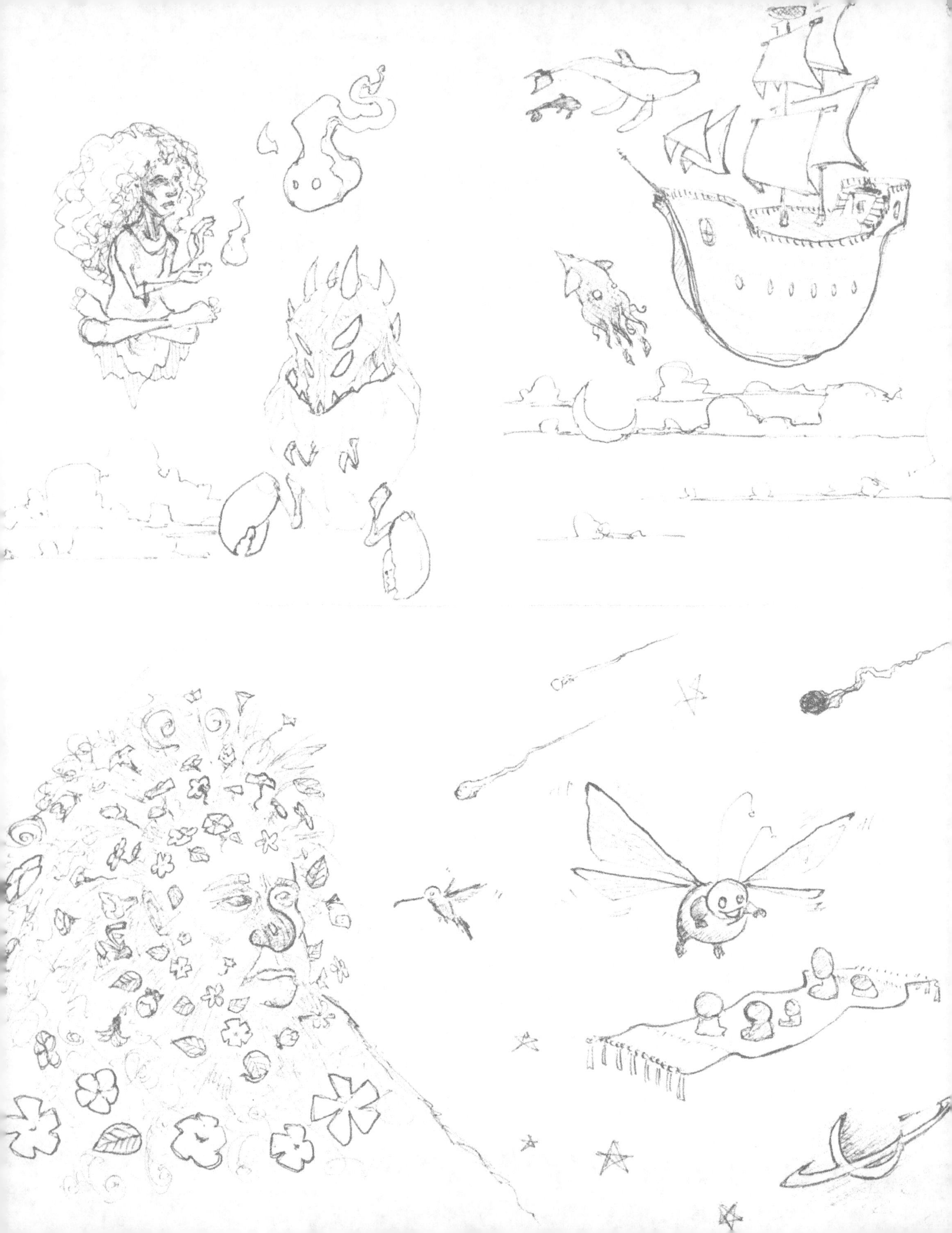

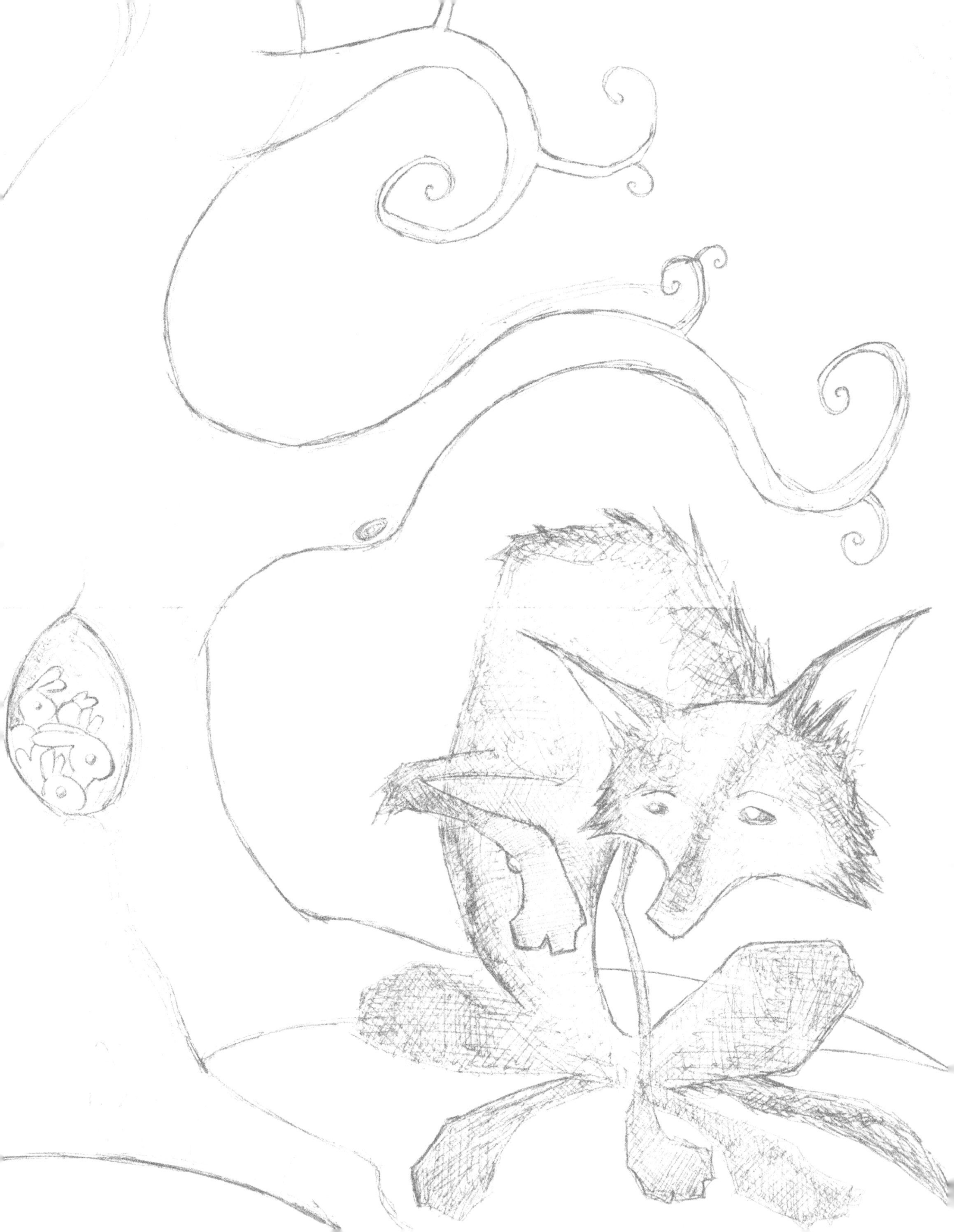

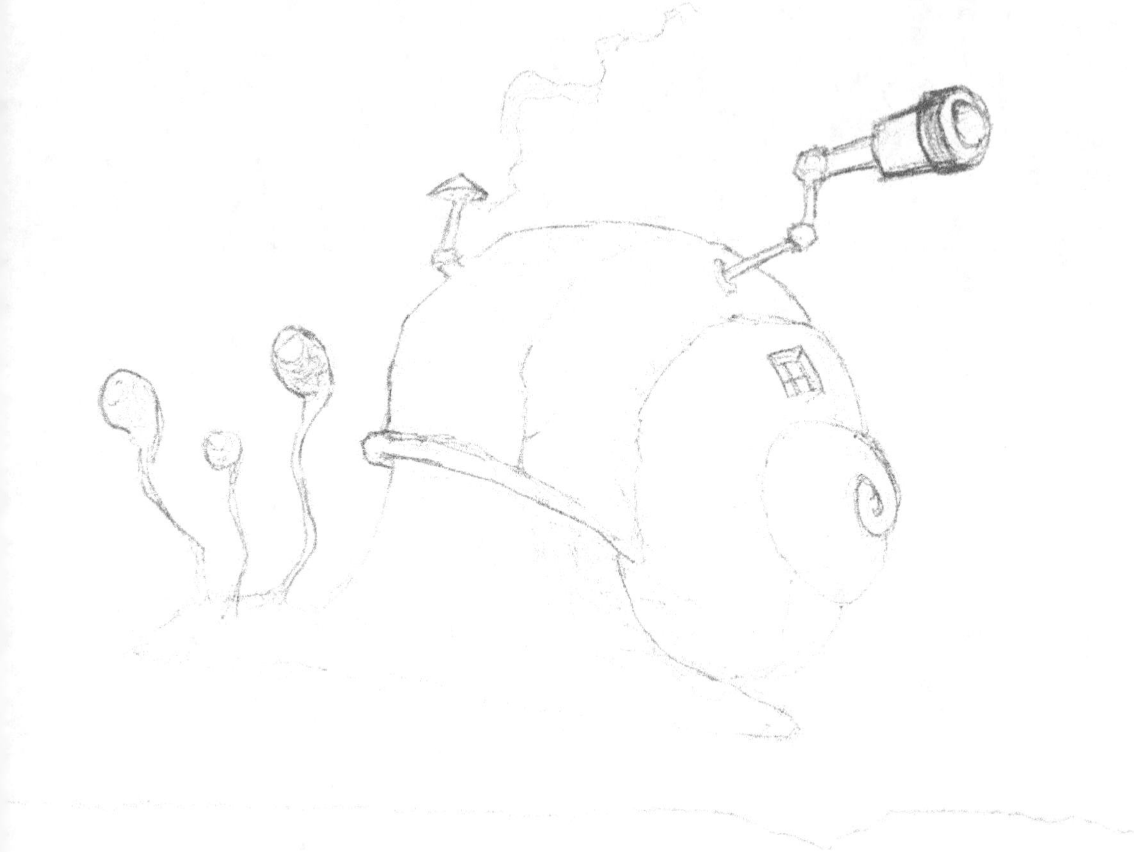

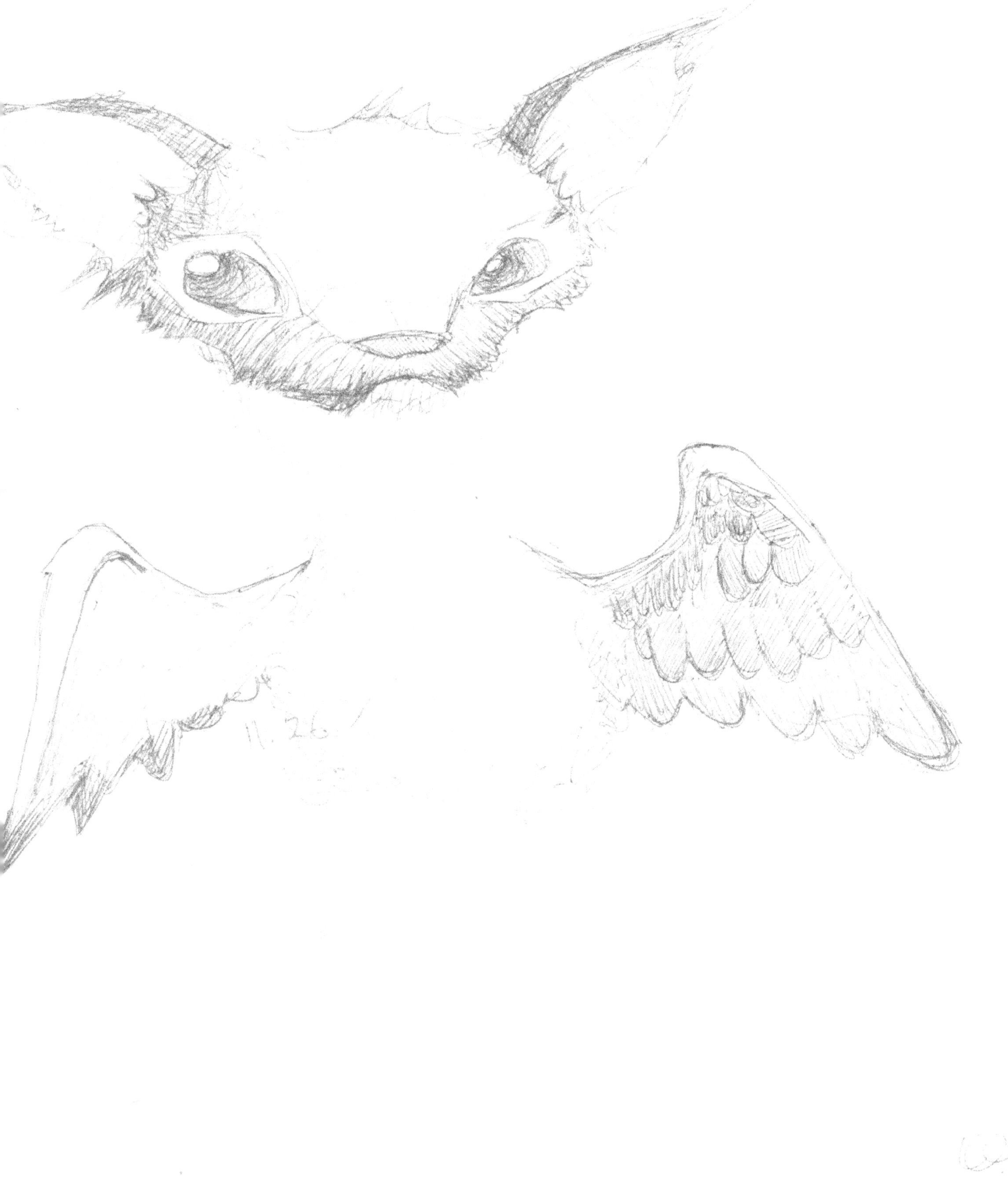
11.26

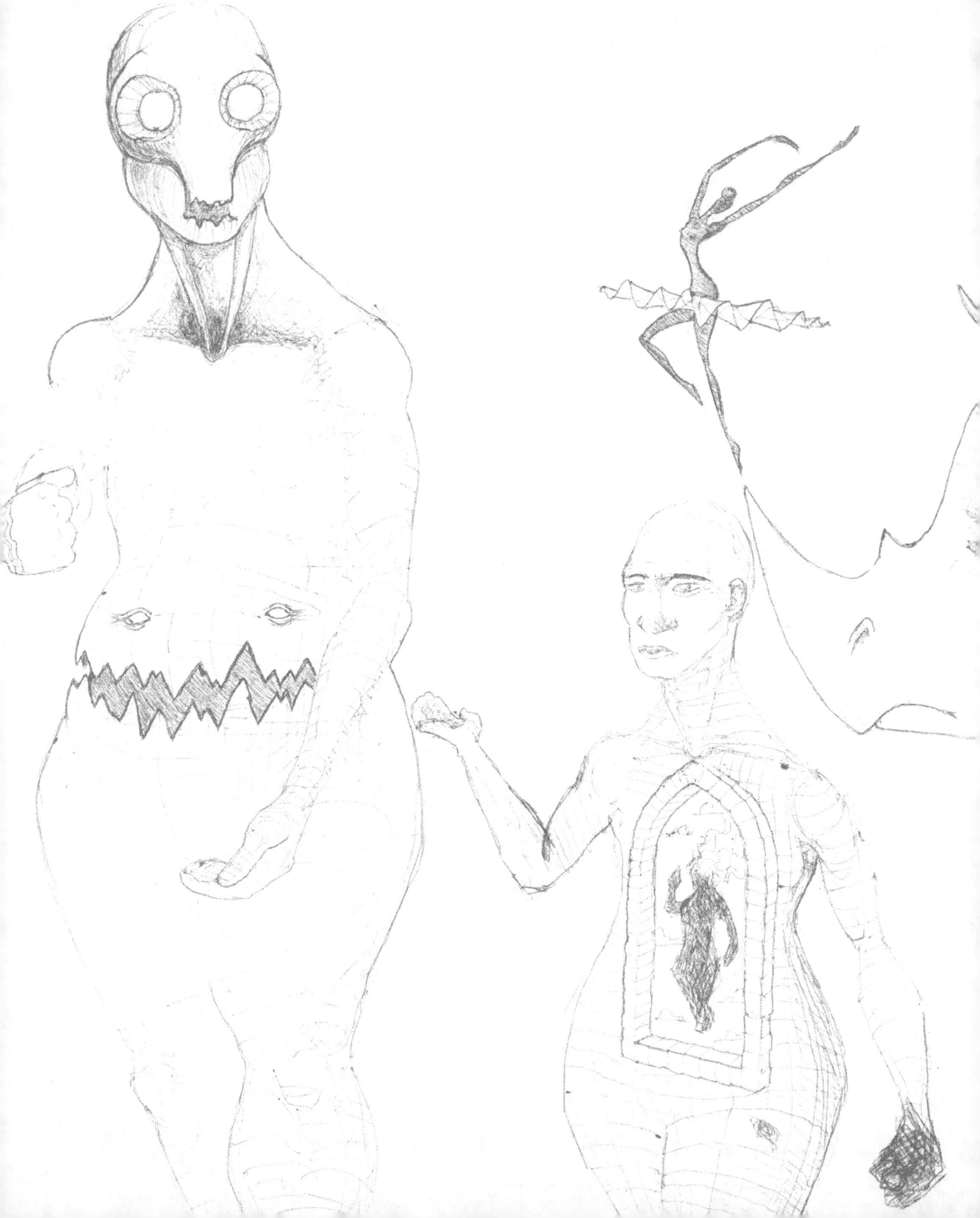

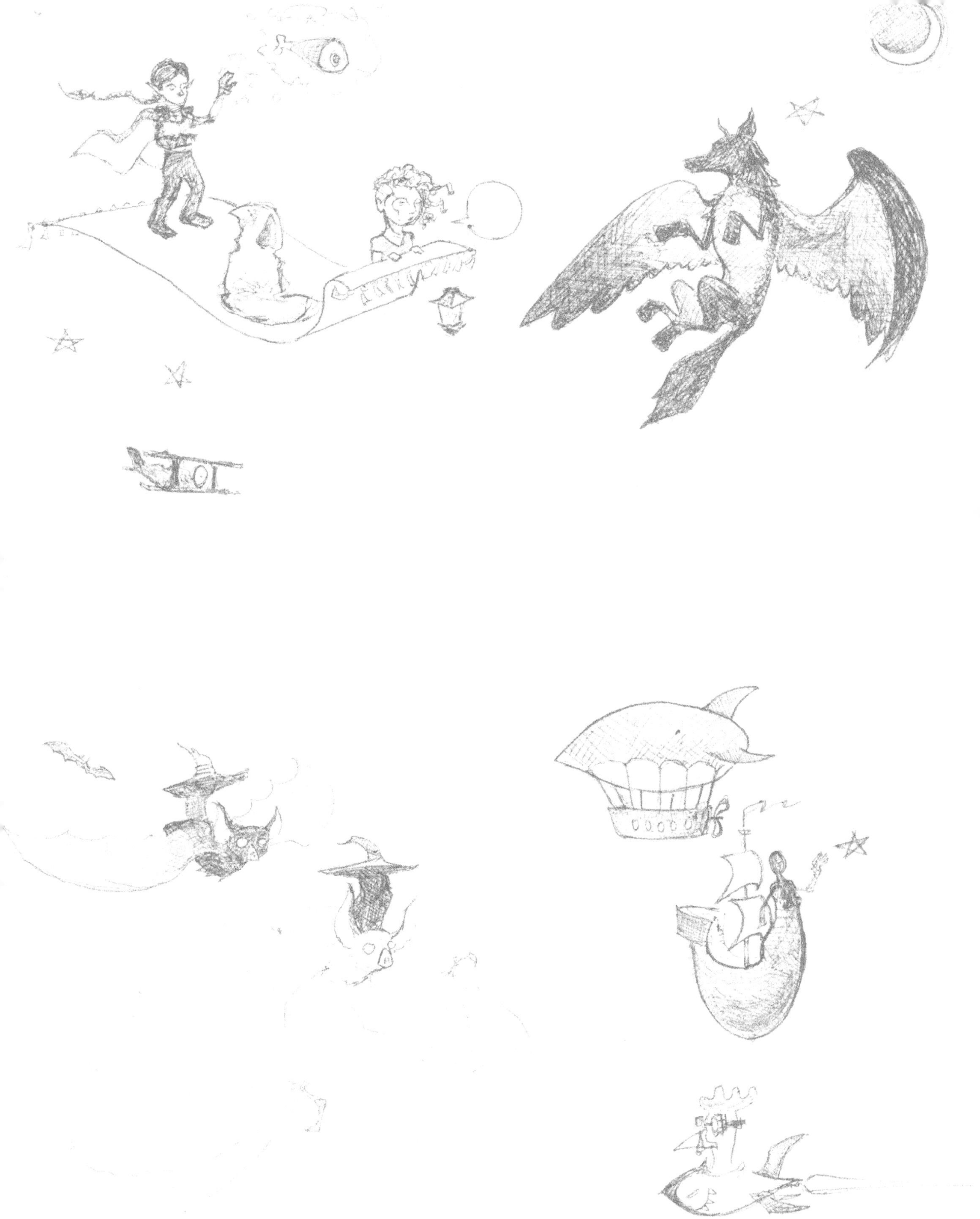

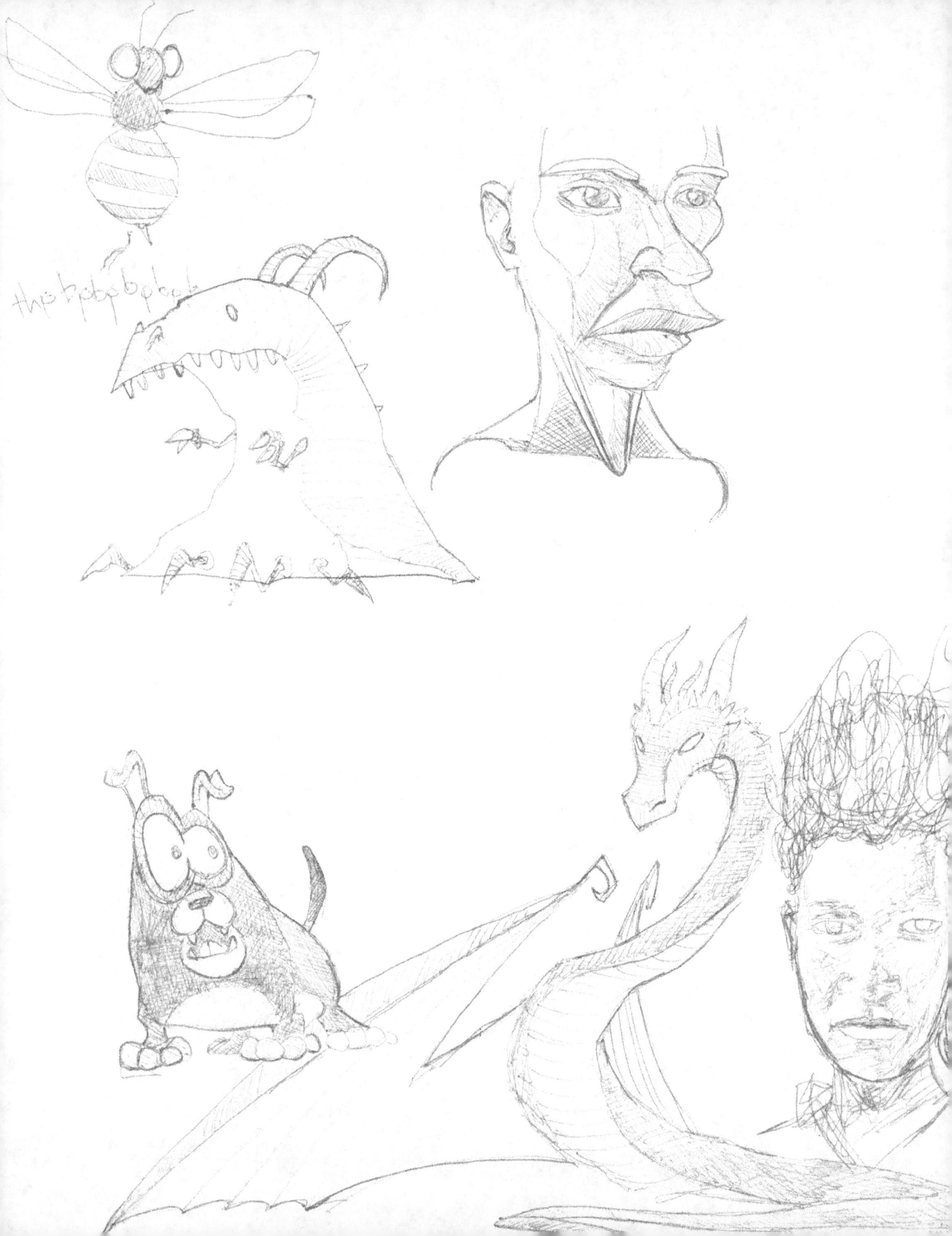

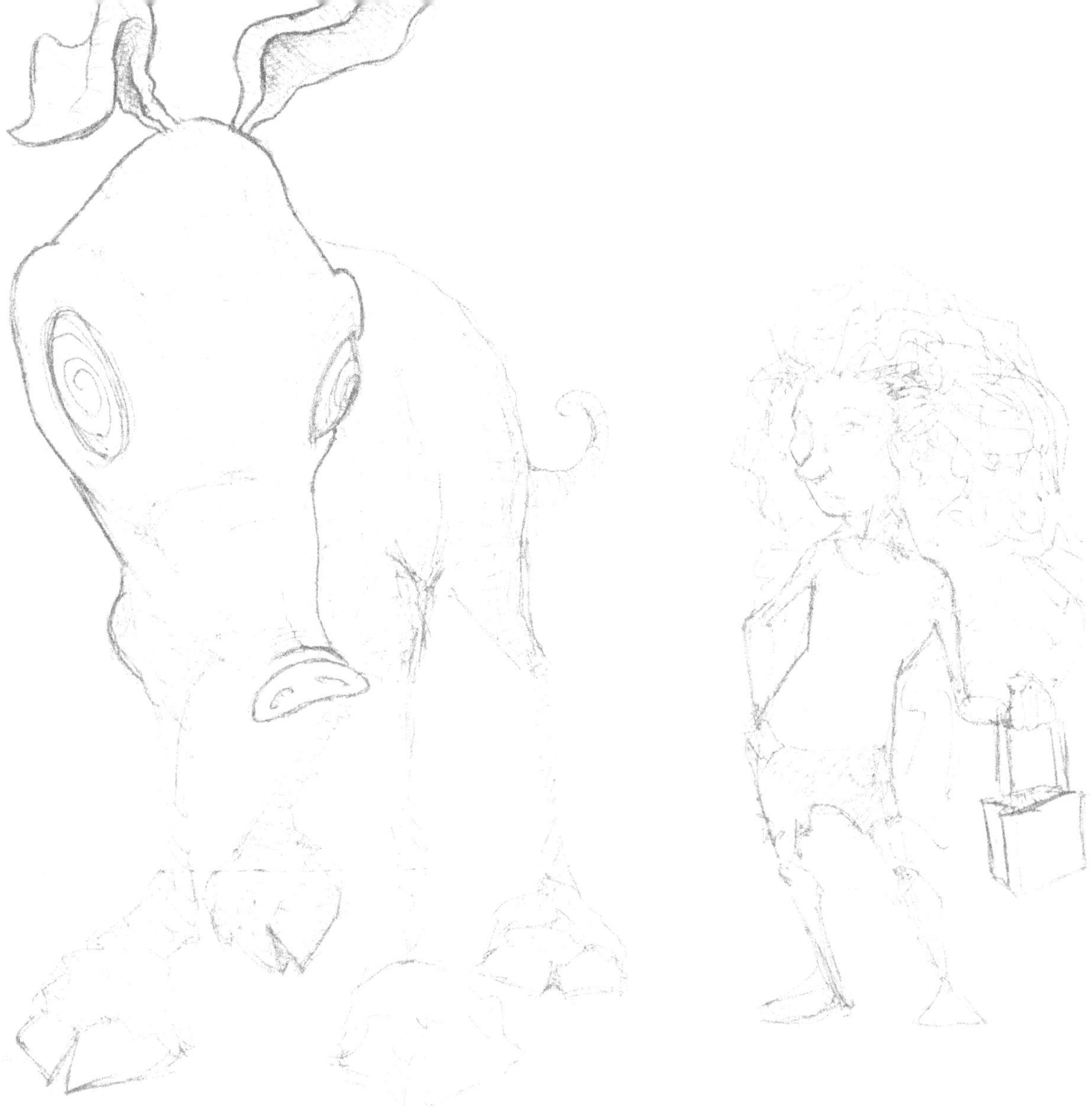

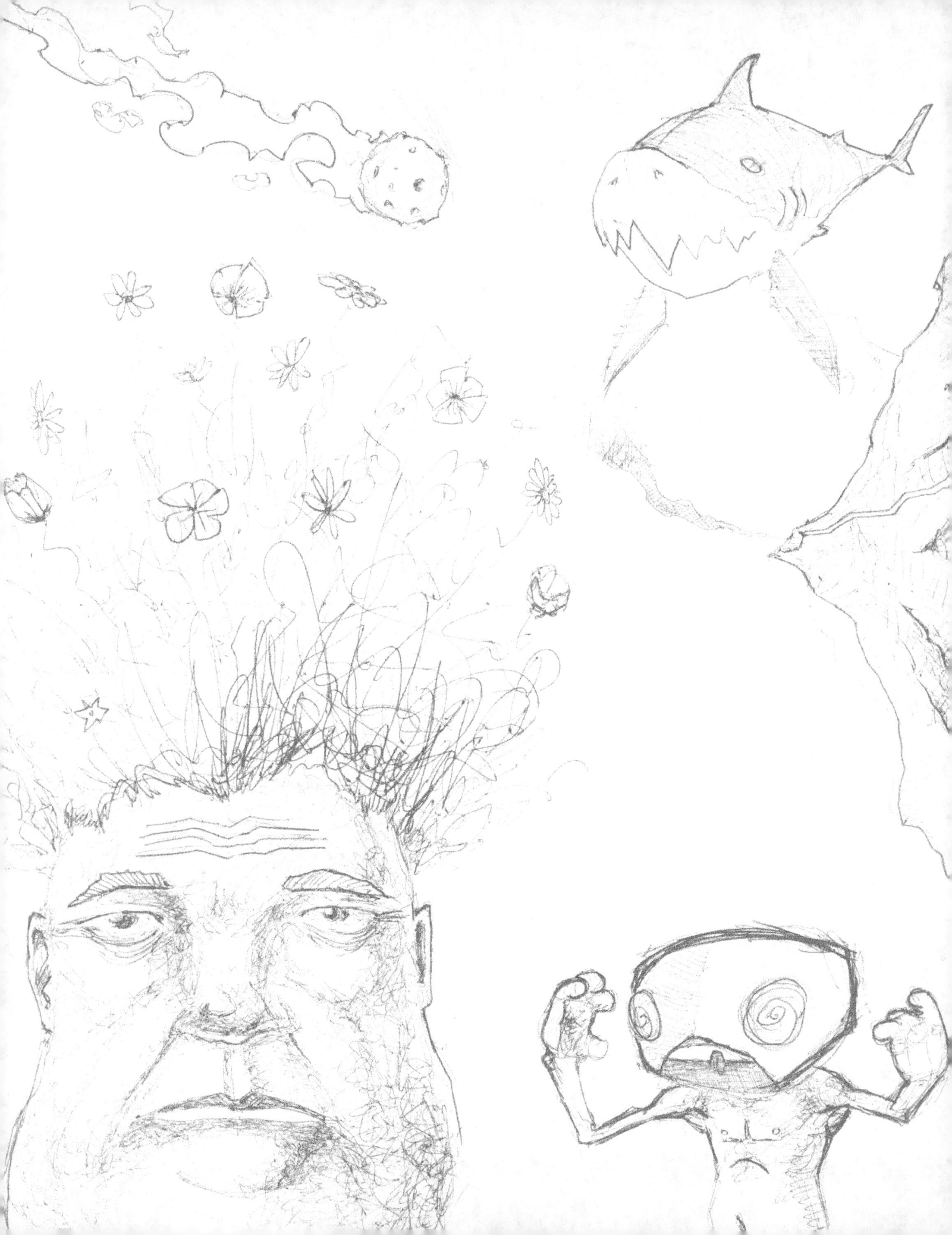

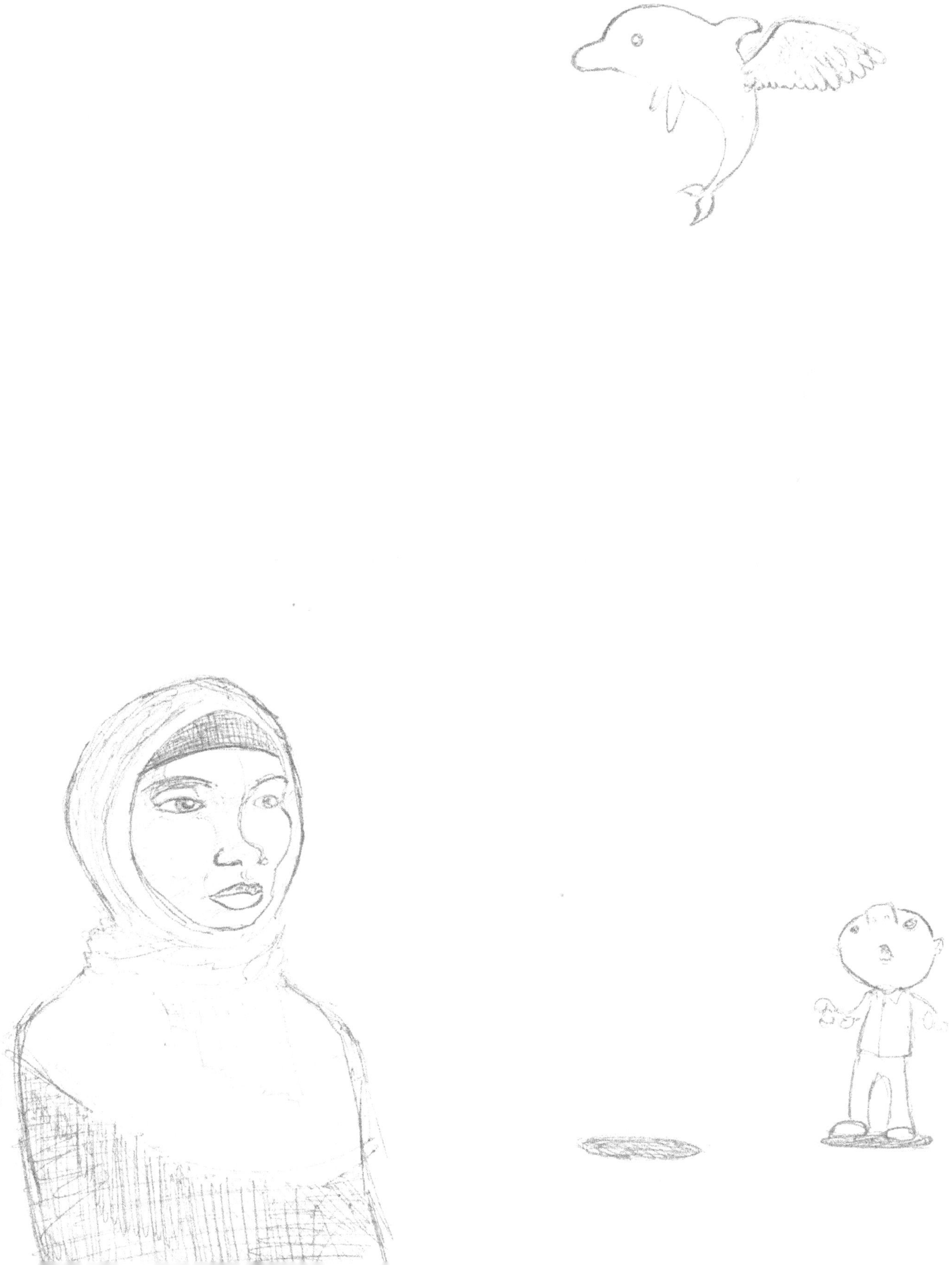

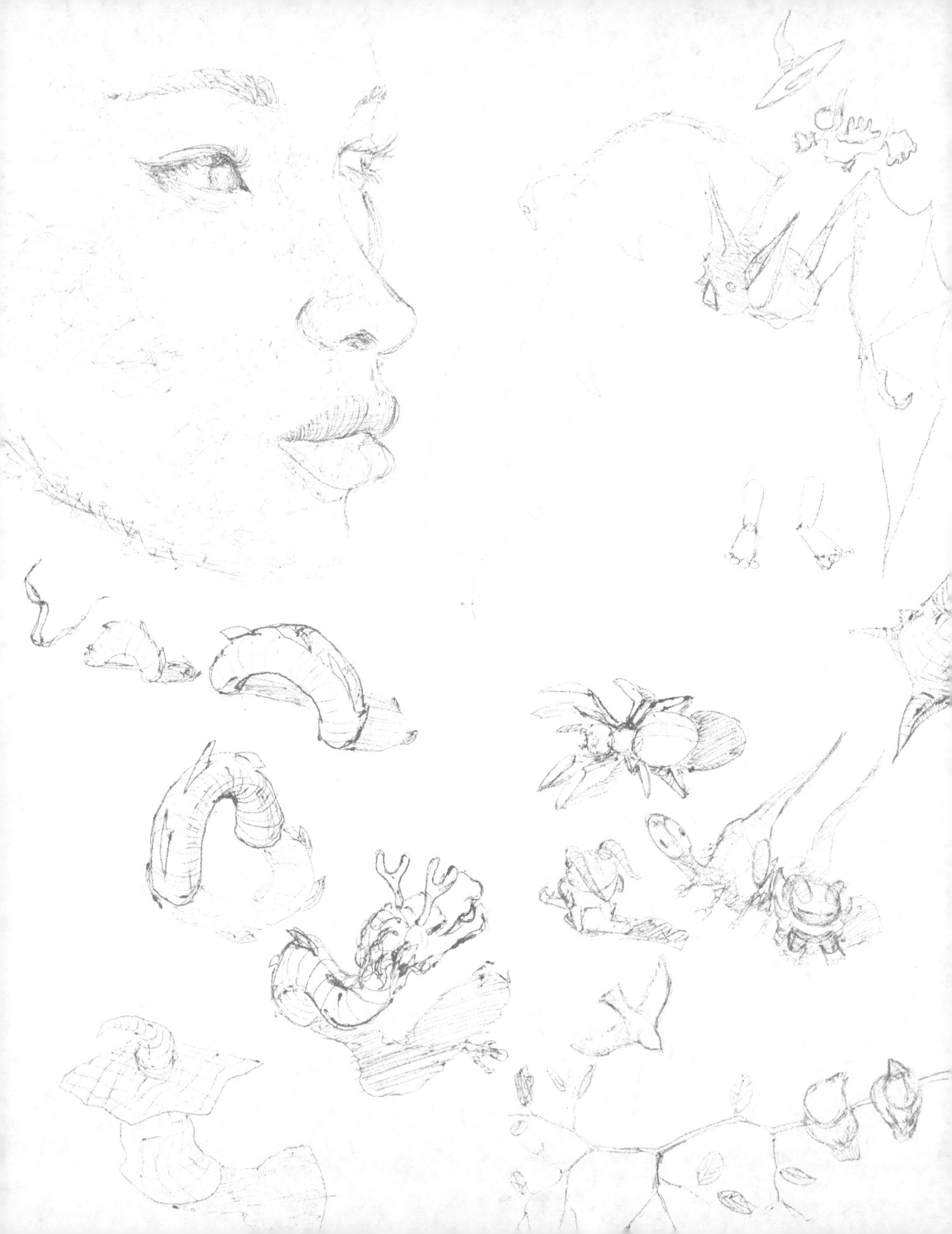

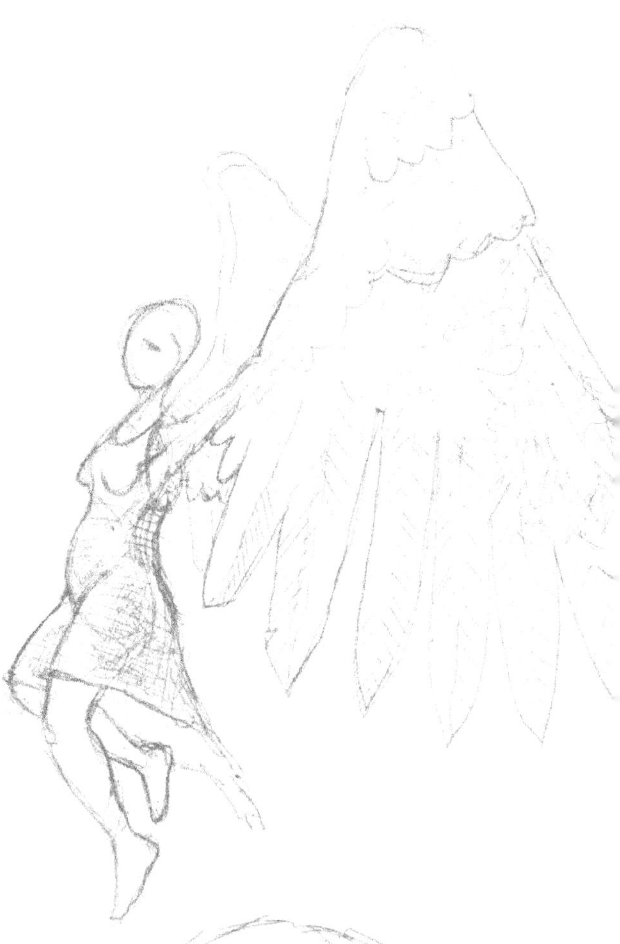

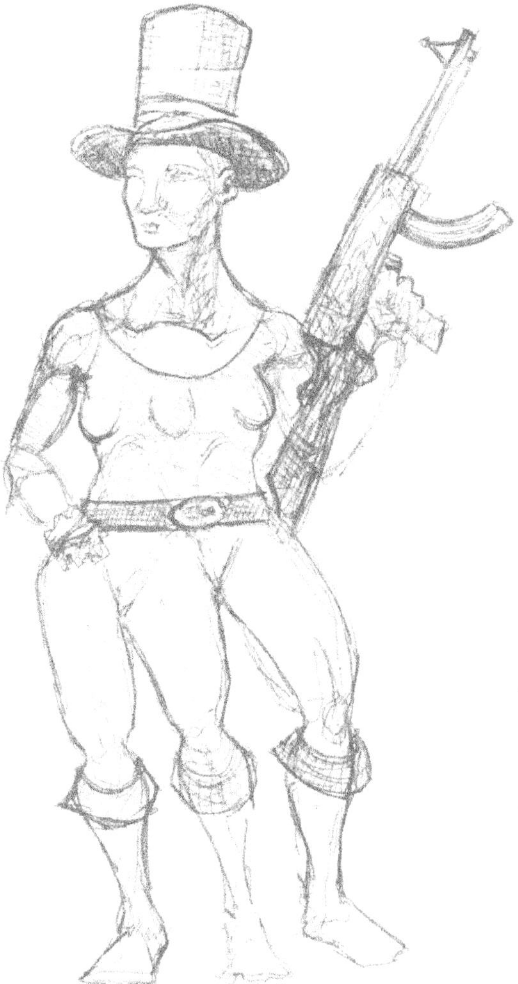

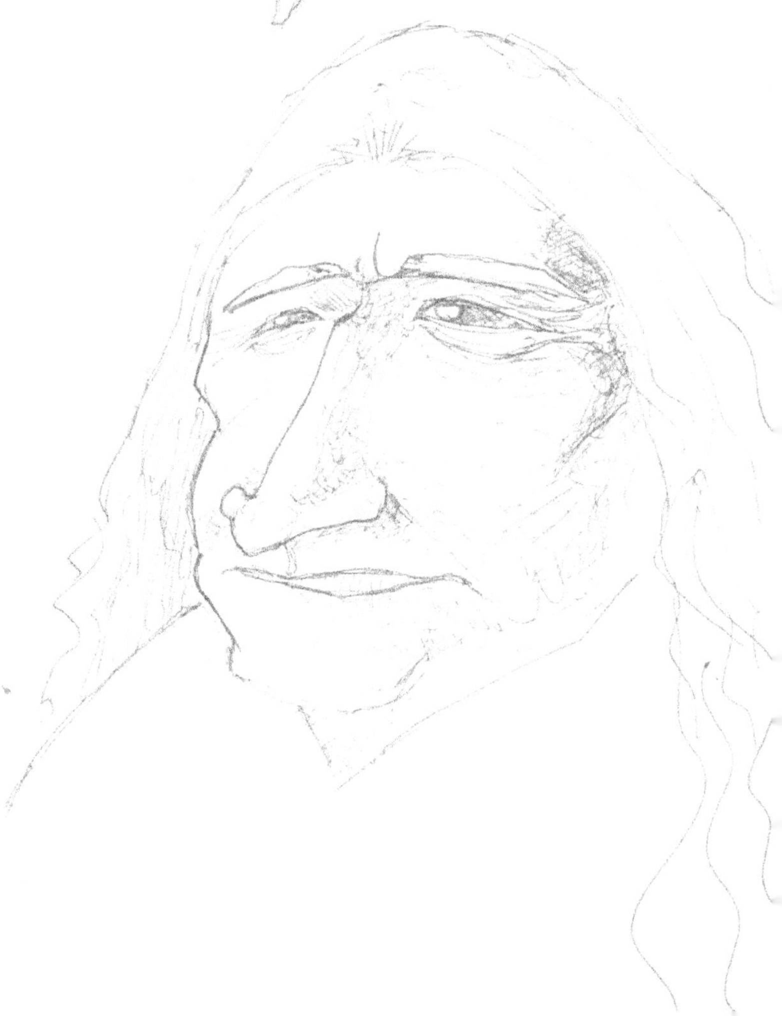

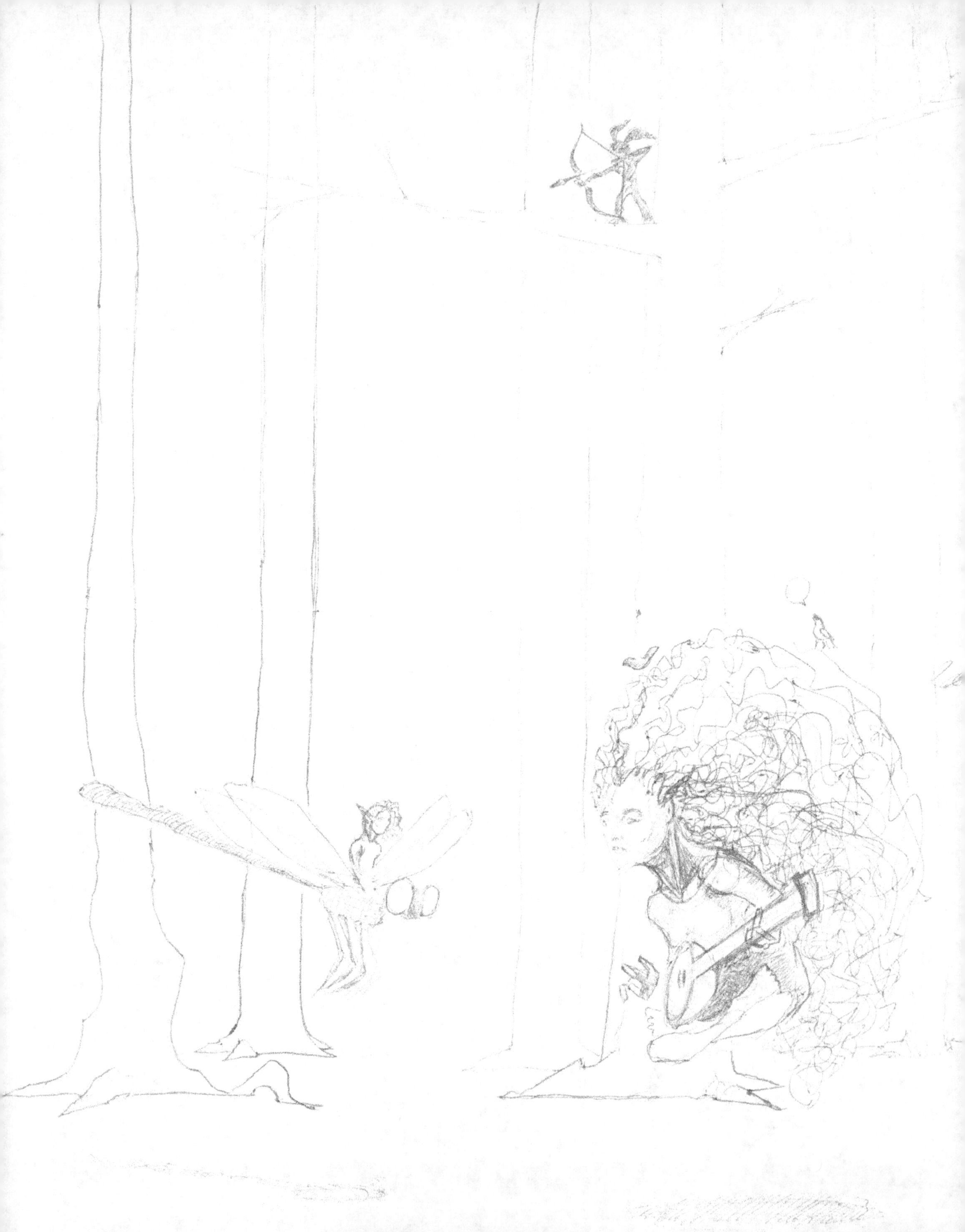

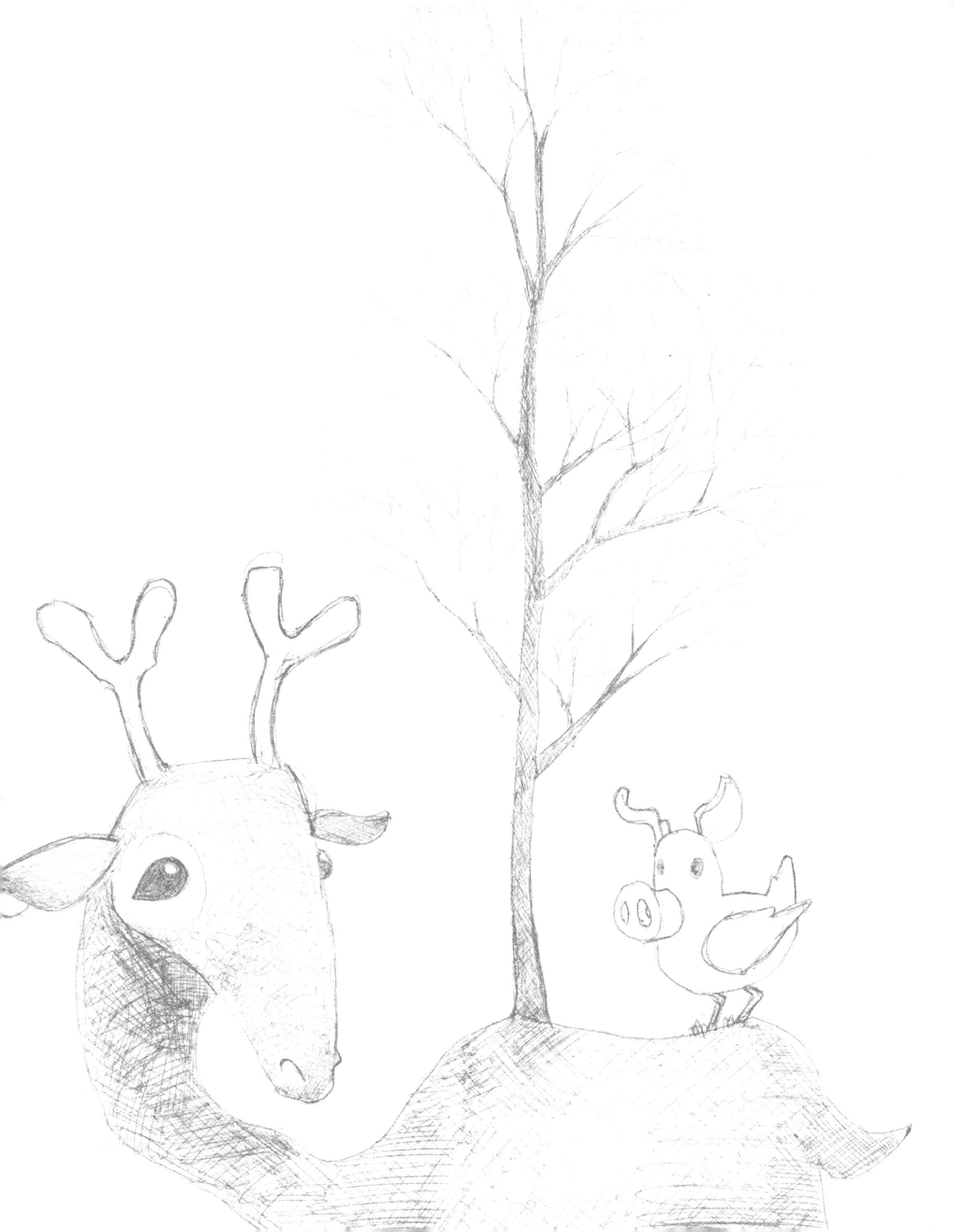

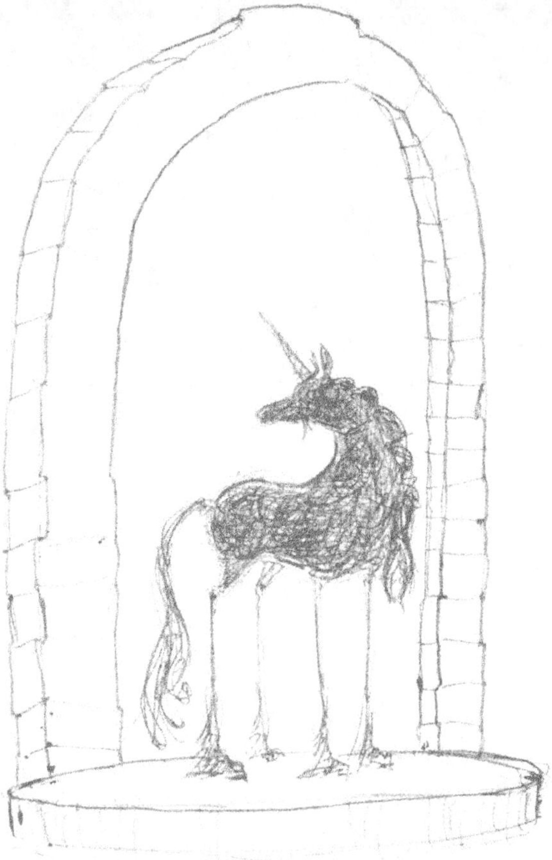

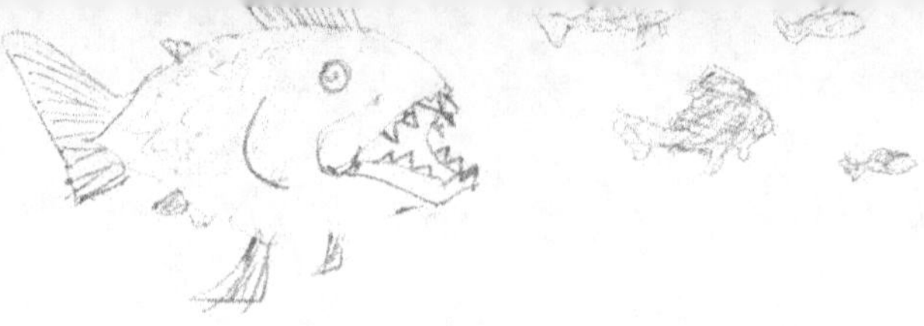

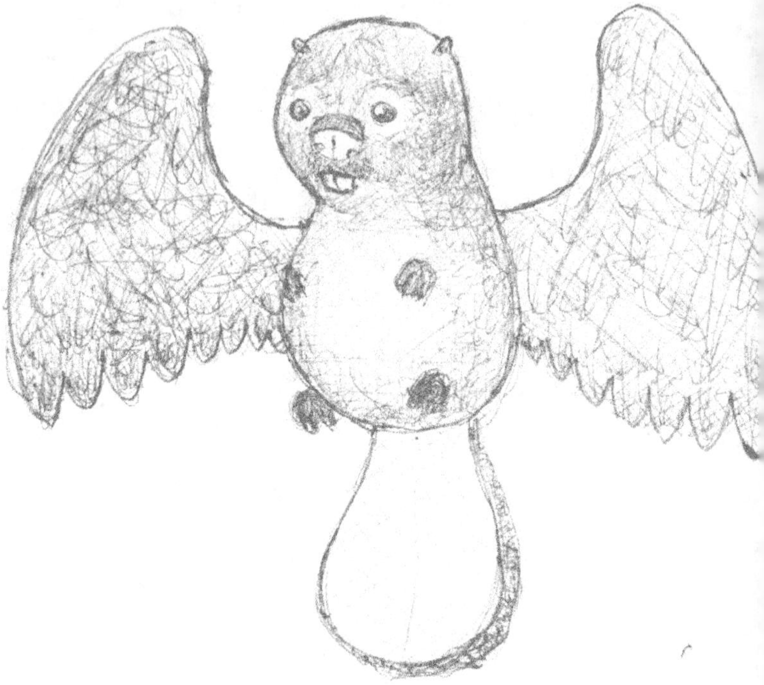

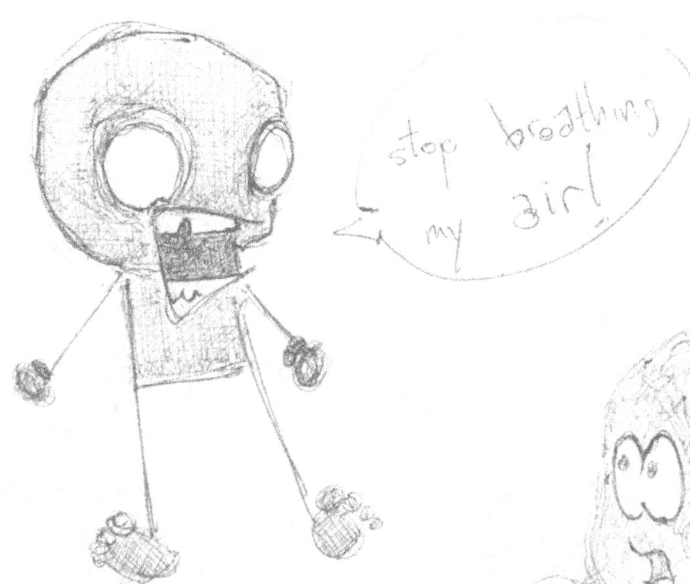
stop breathing my air!

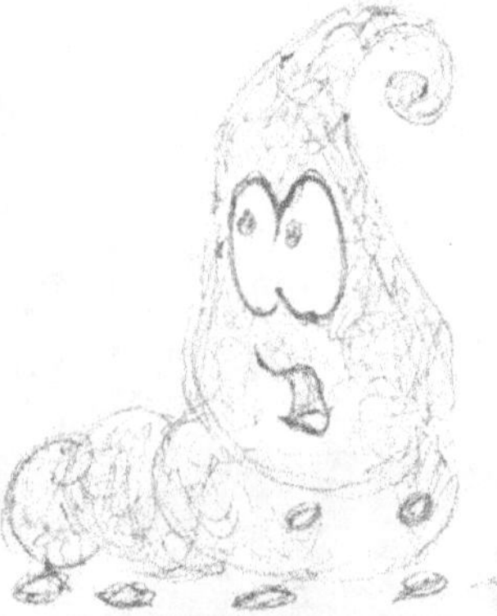

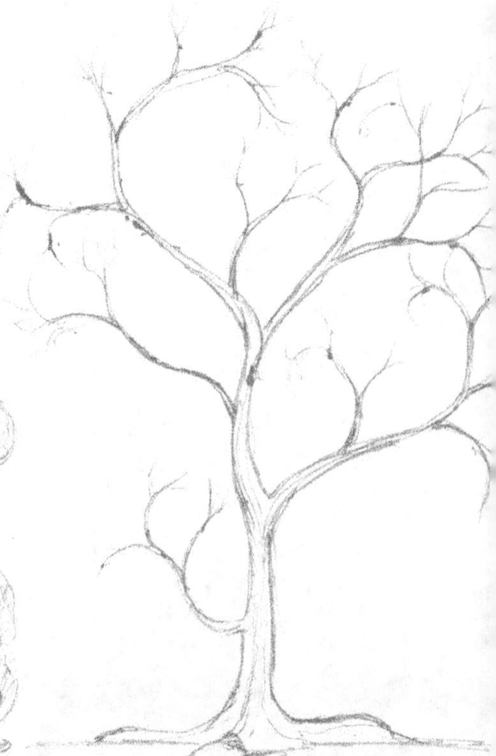

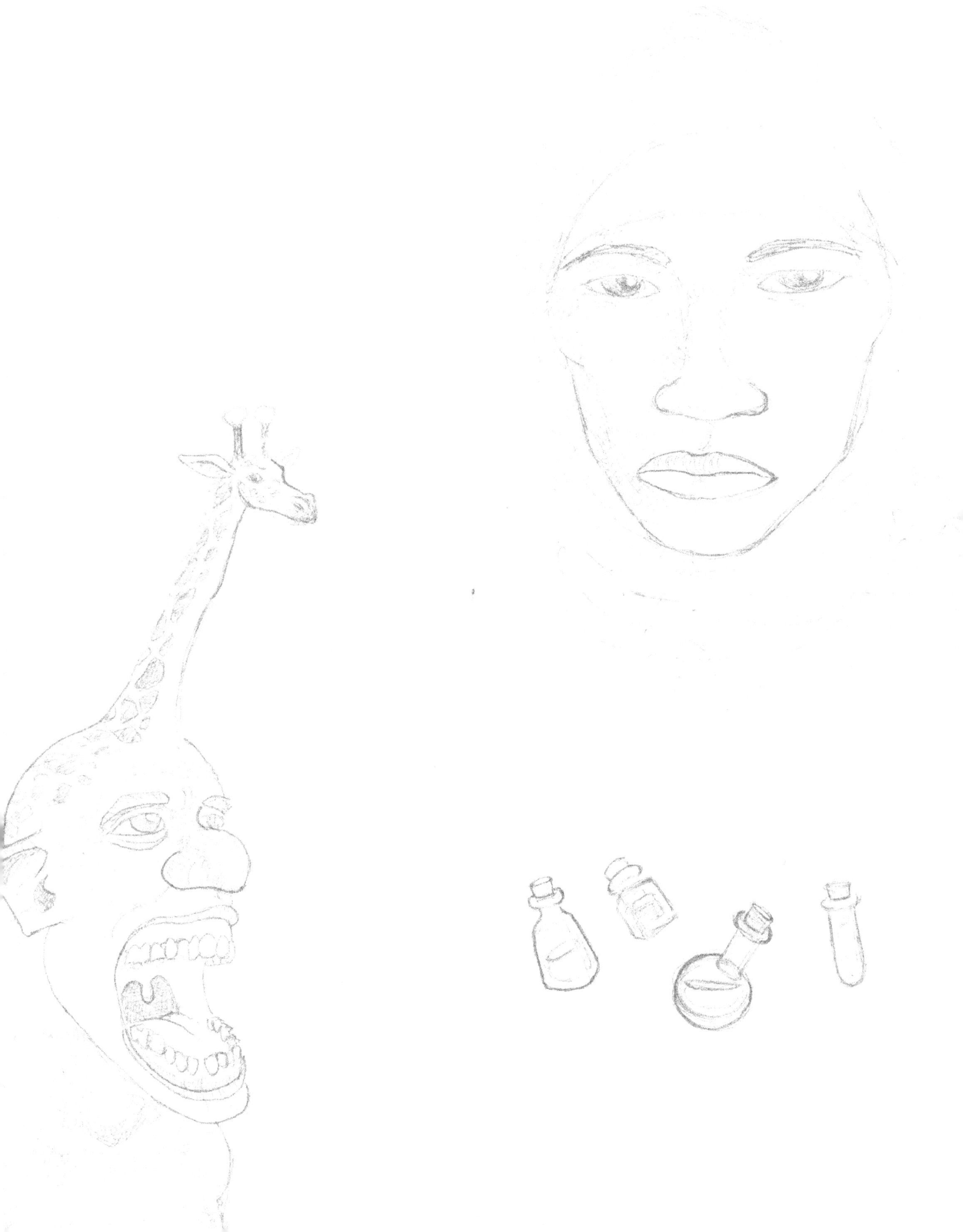

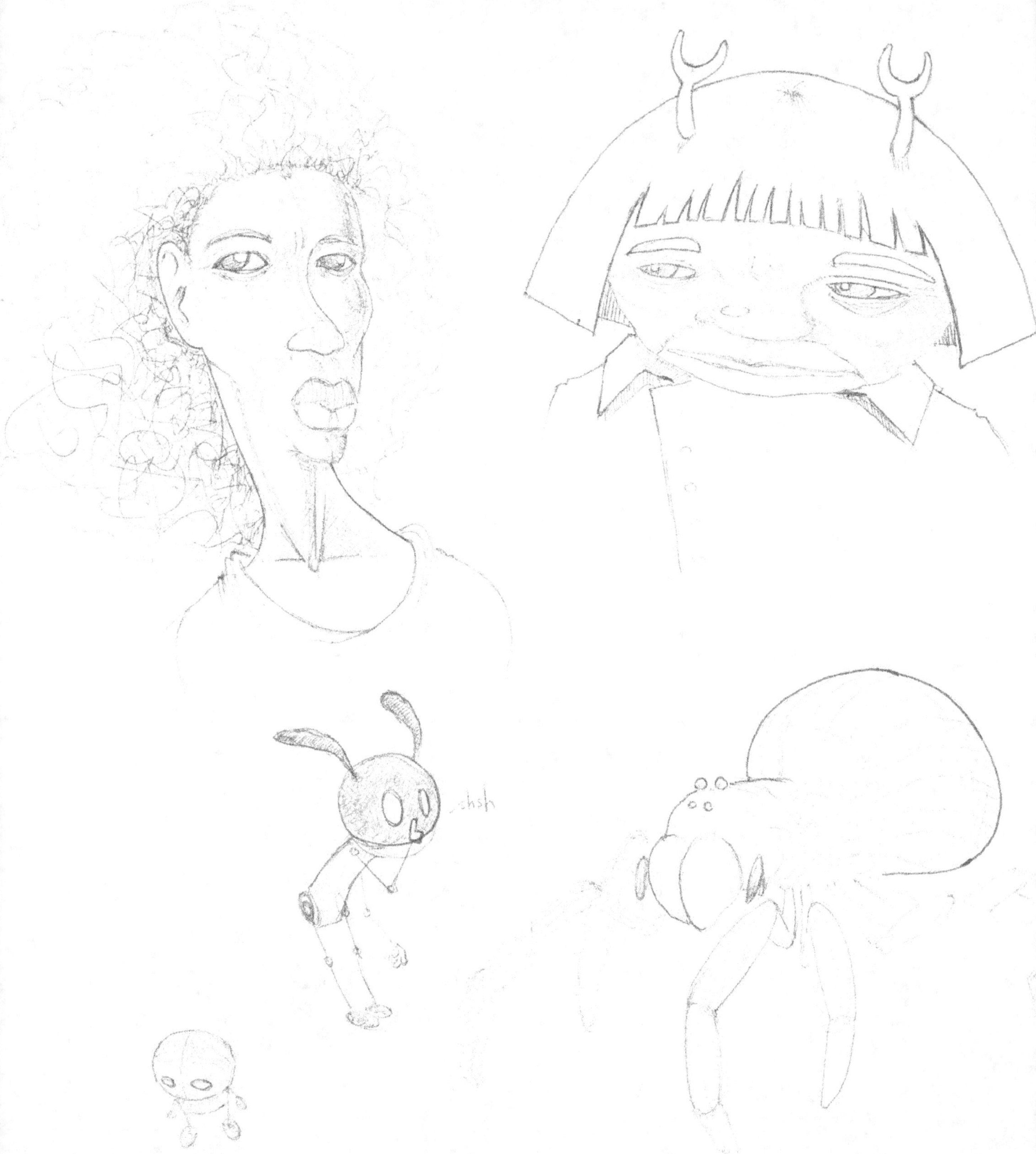
shsh

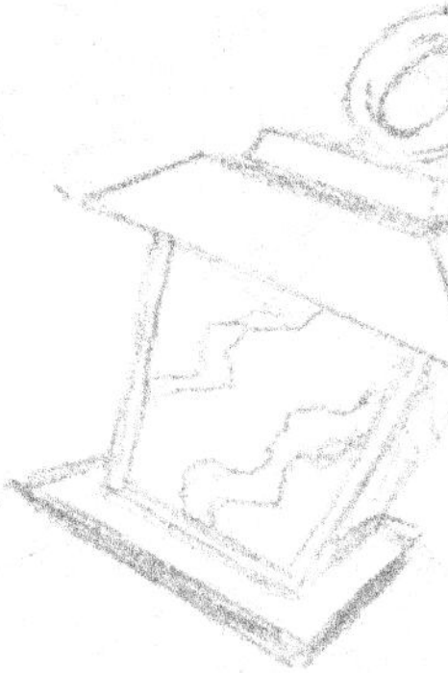

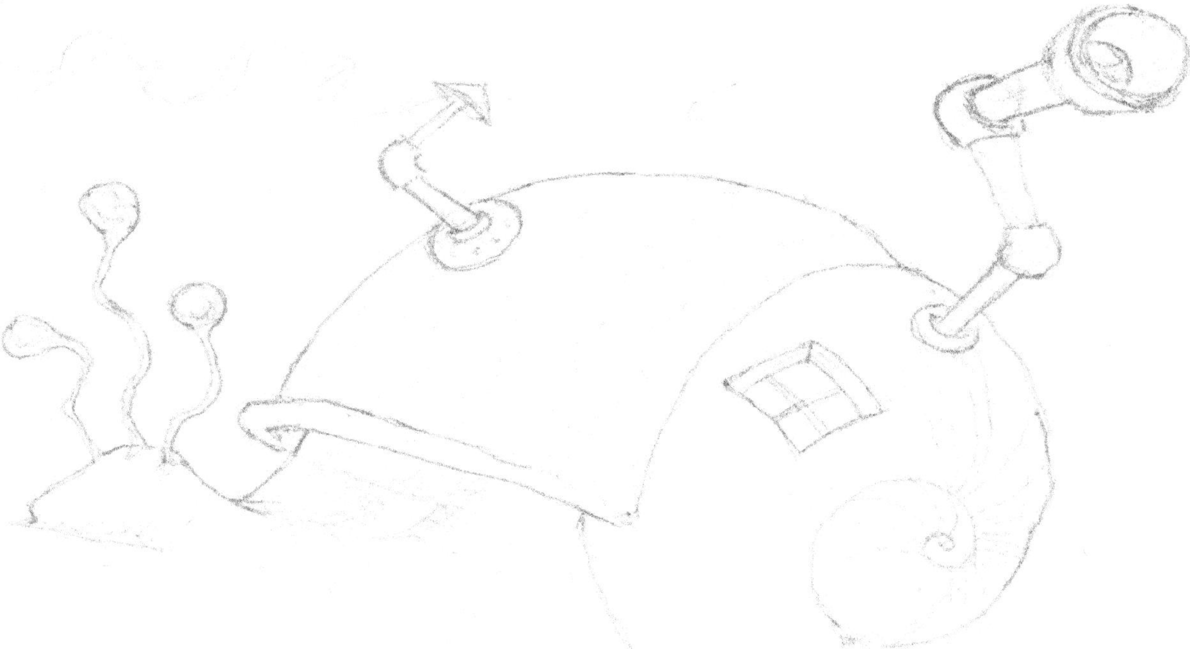

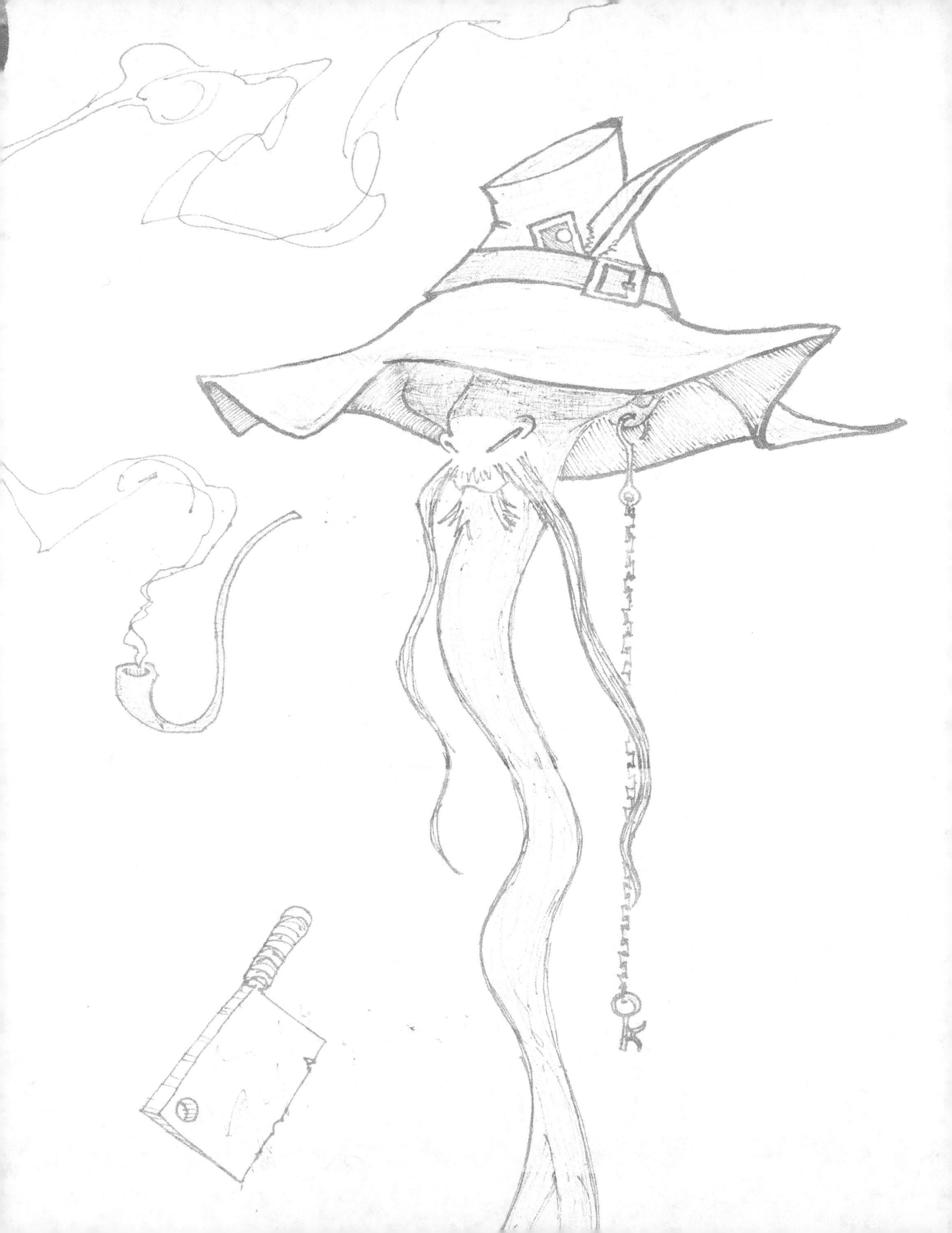

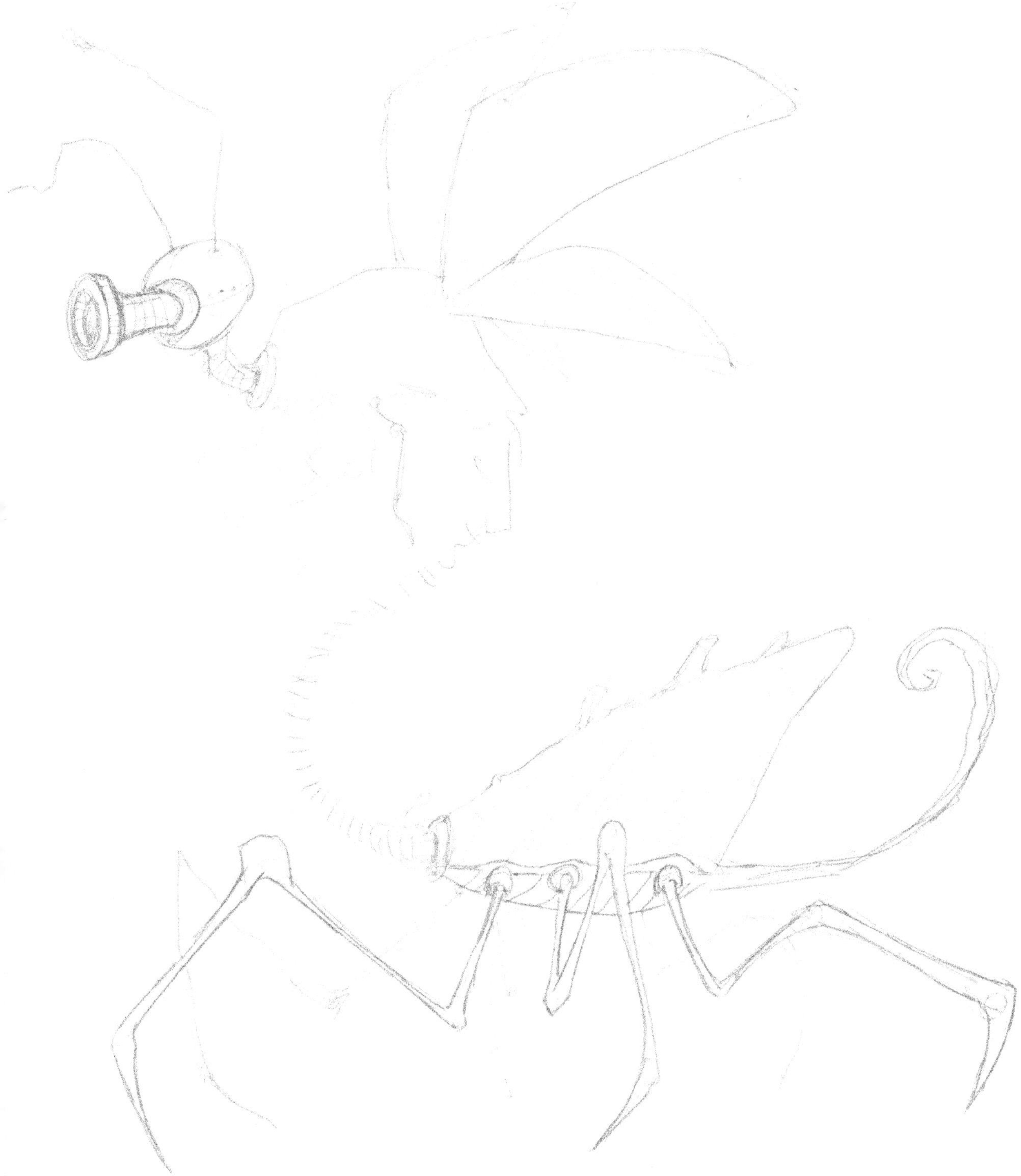

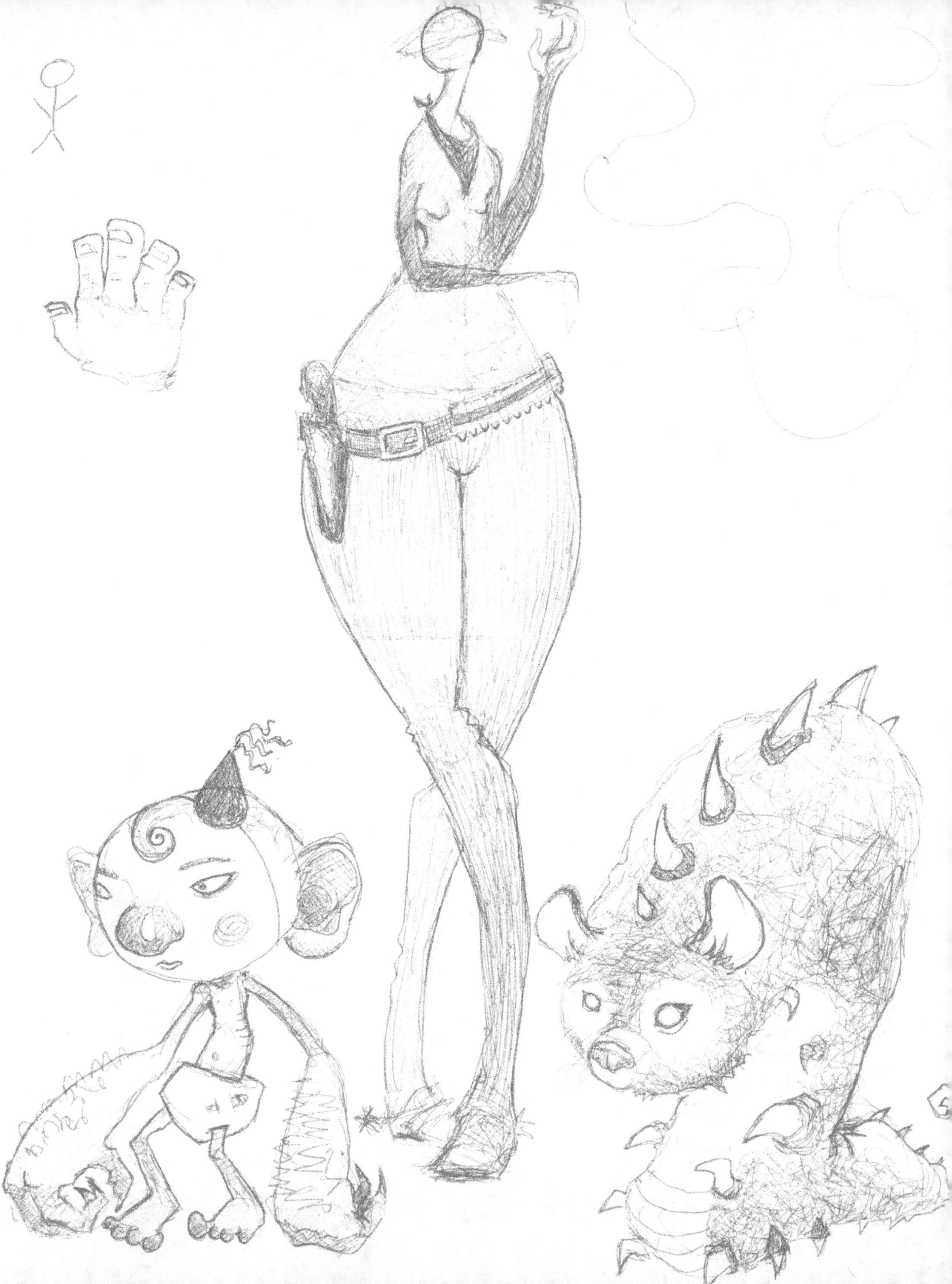

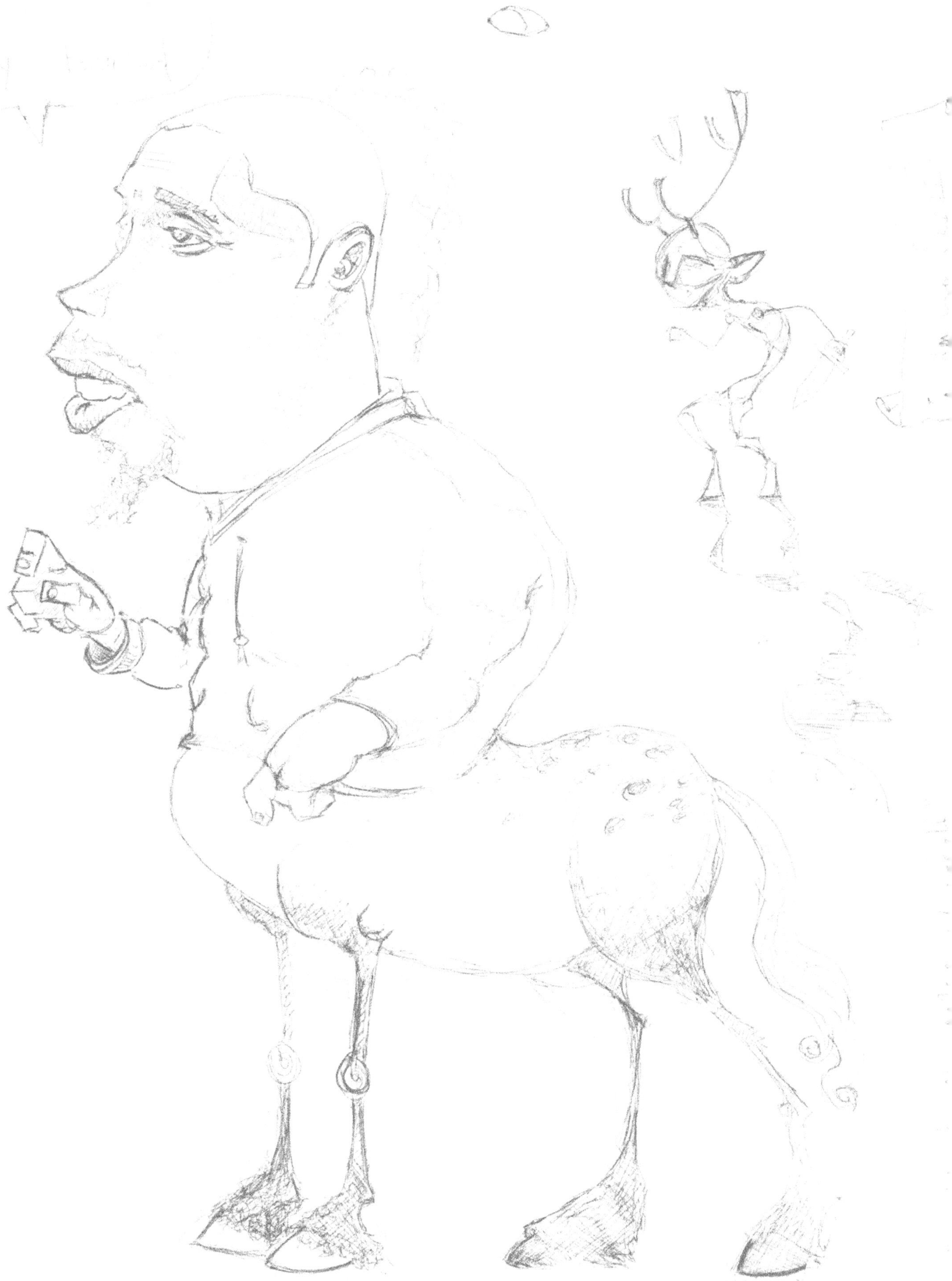

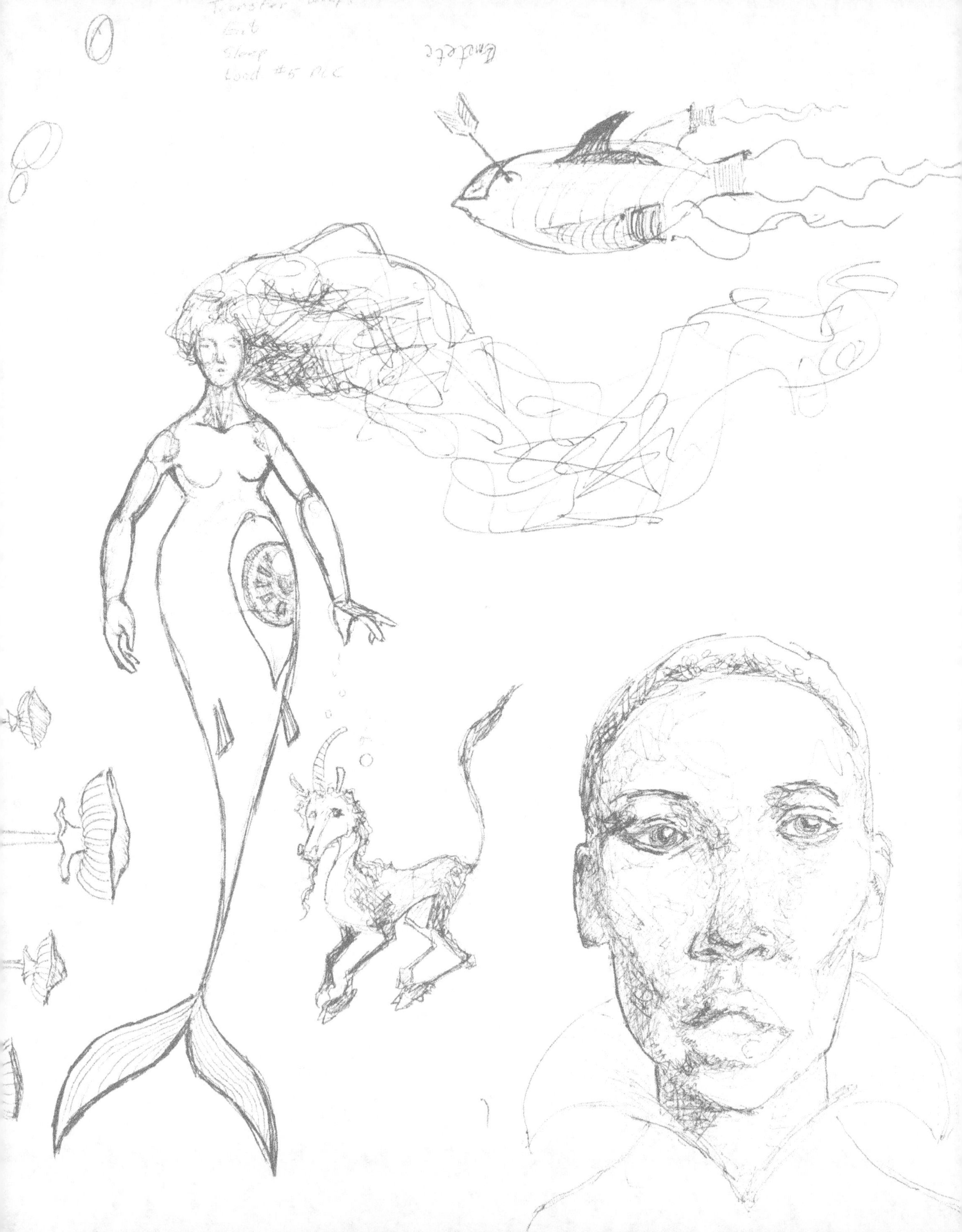
Transfer
Eat
Sleep
Load #5

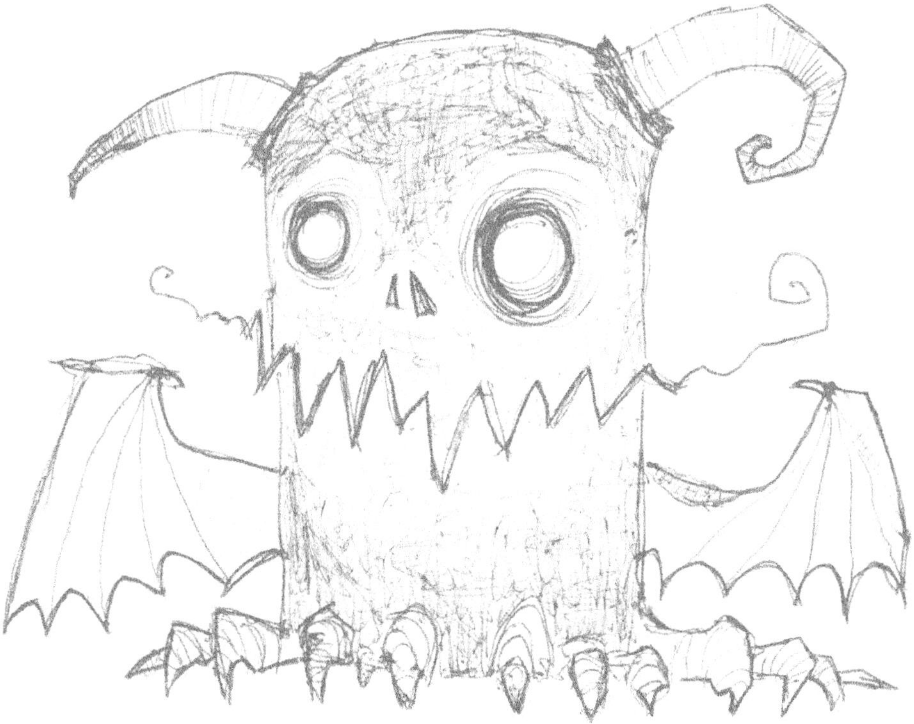

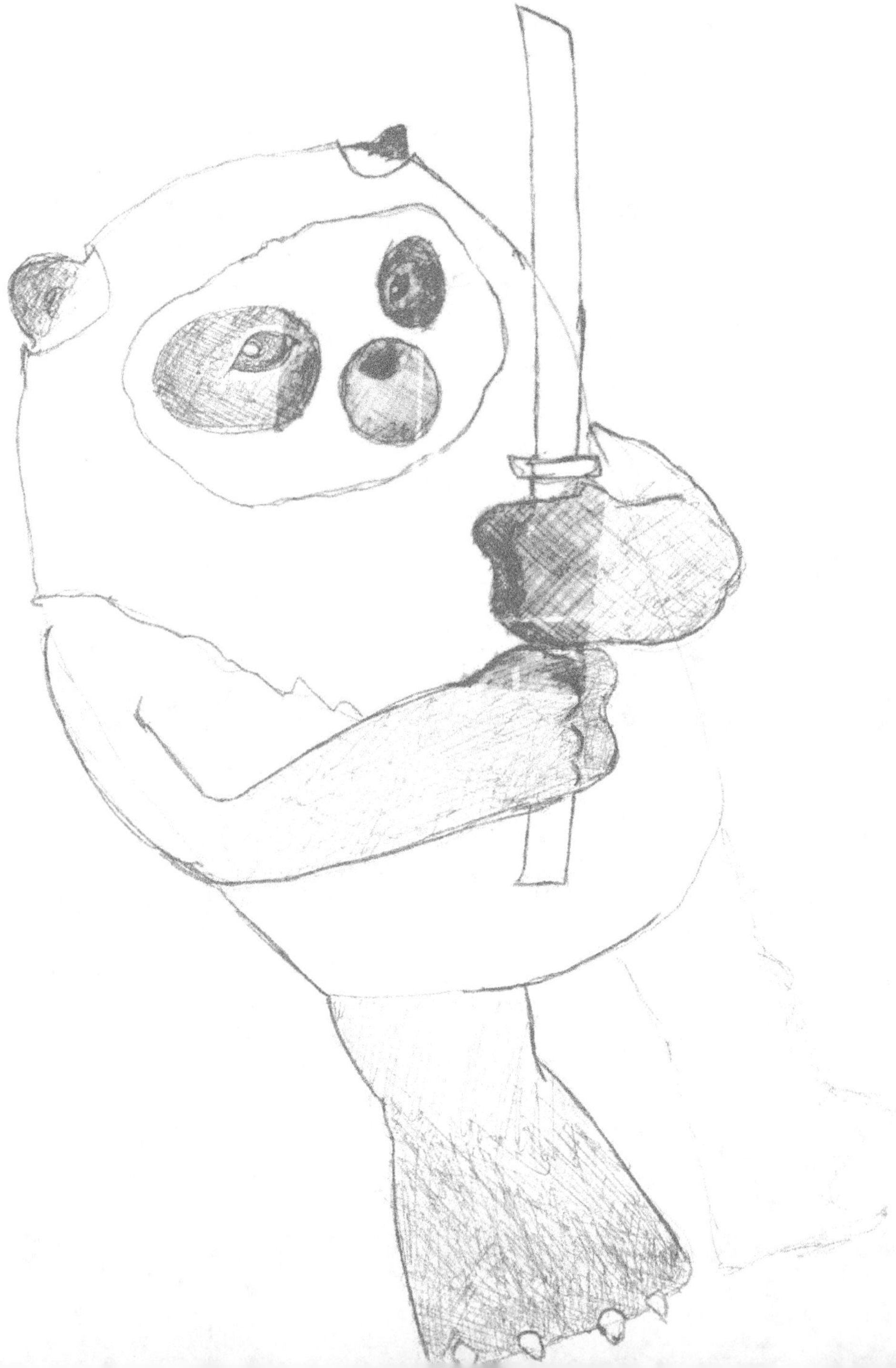

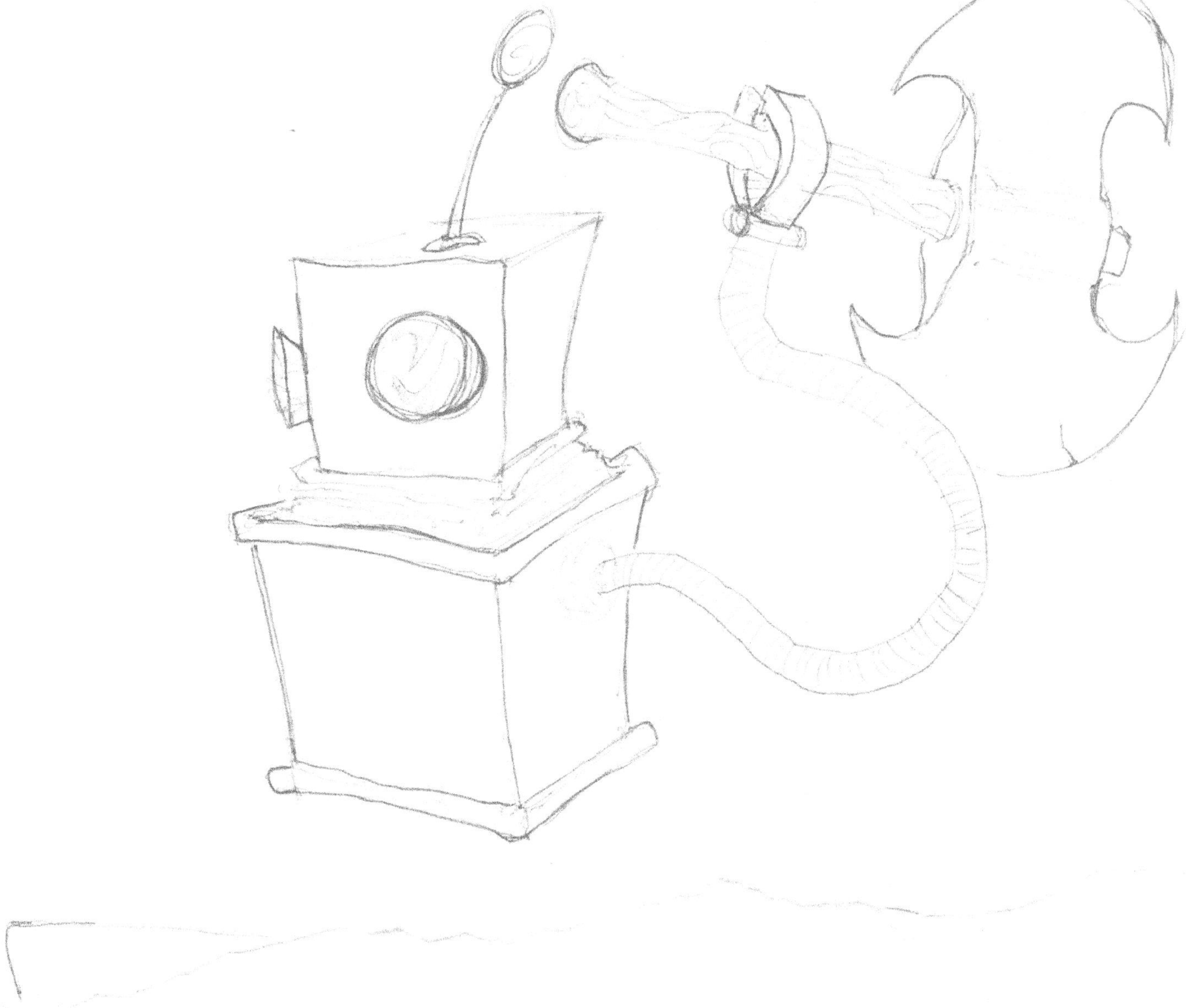

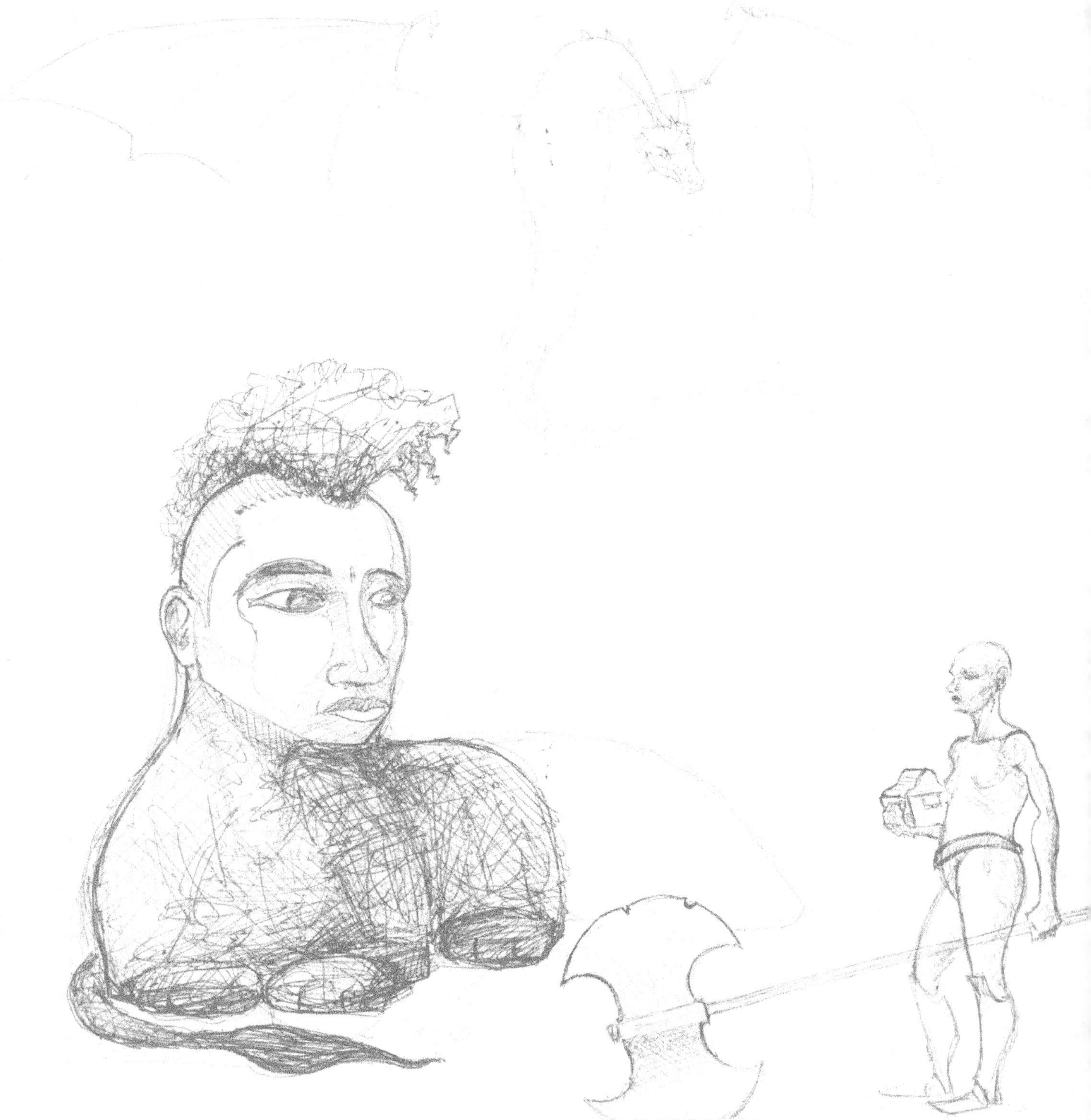

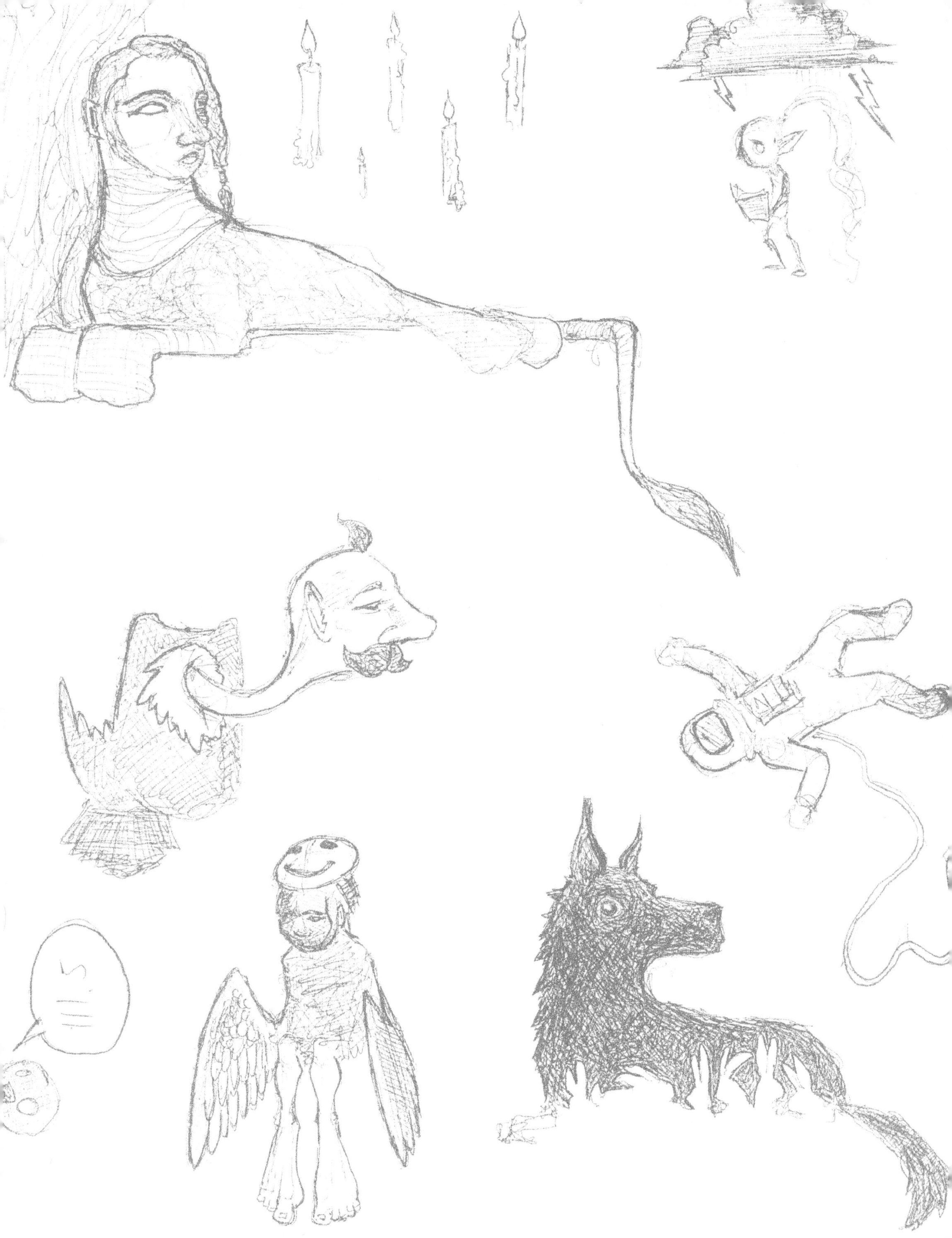

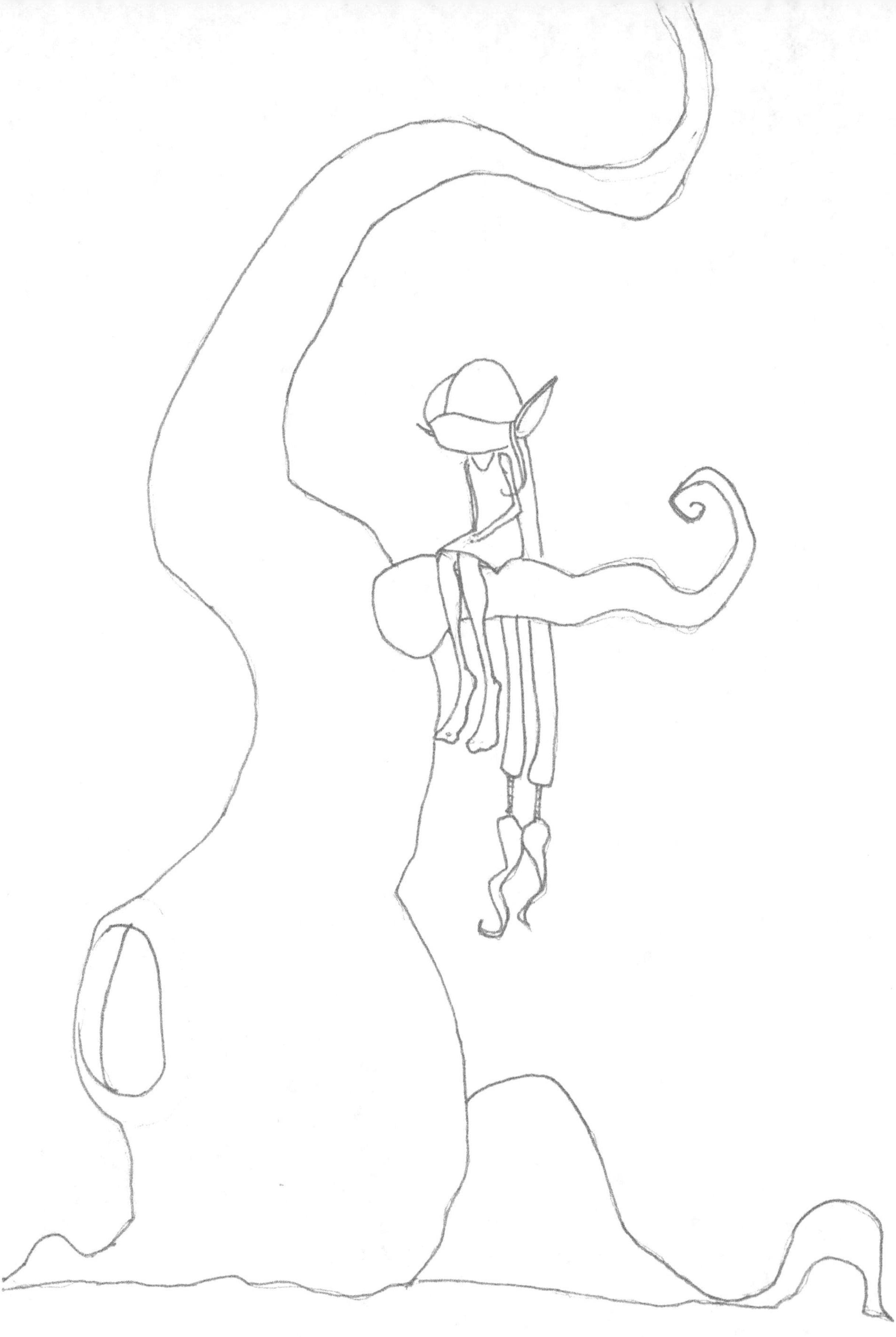

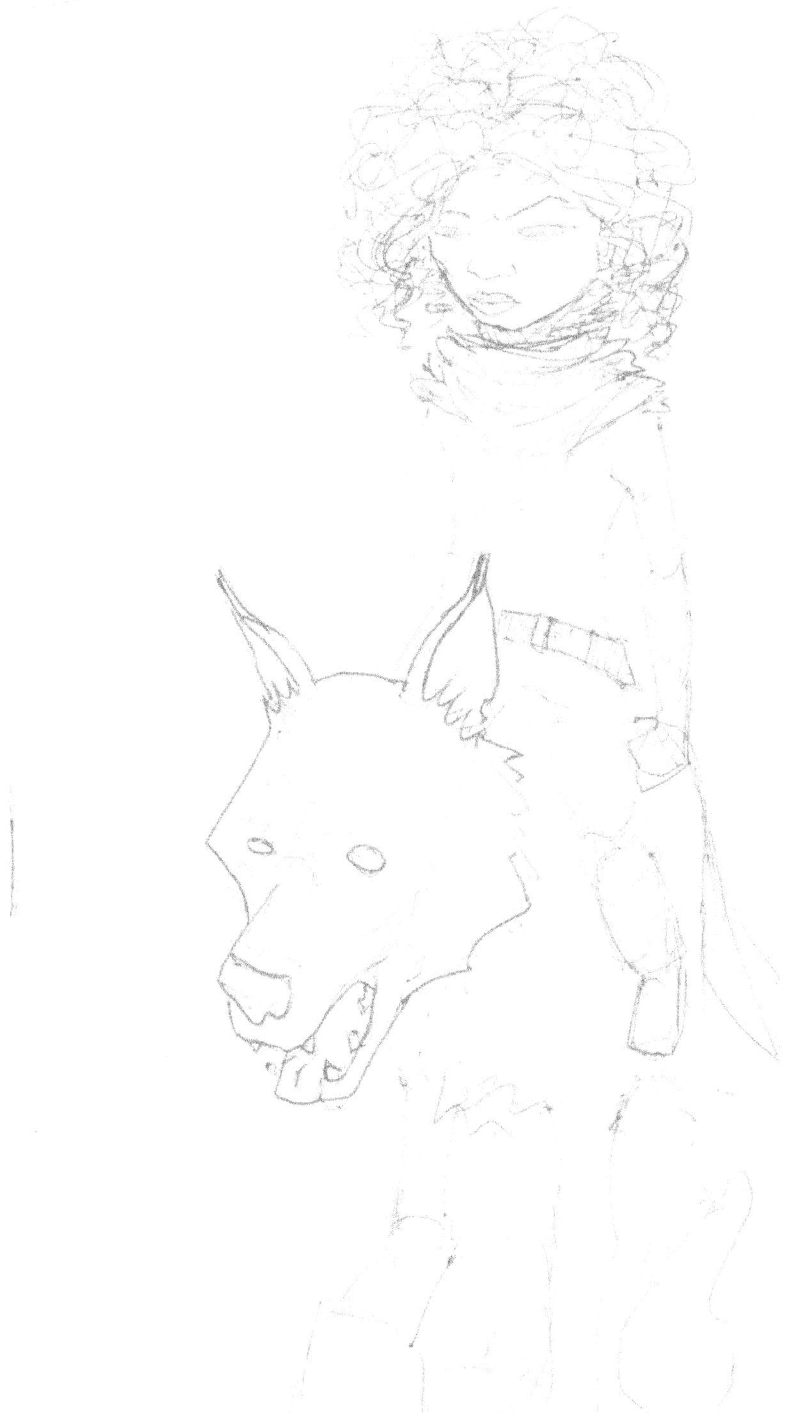

www.ingramcontent.com/pod-product-compliance
Lightning Source LLC
Chambersburg PA
CBHW080538190526
45169CB00007B/2544
* 9 7 8 1 5 3 5 0 0 7 8 7 0 *